*To Trish Murphy
to a great bonsai hobbiest
With my best wishes!
Bill*

Classical Bonsai Art
A Half Century of Bonsai Study

The Creations & Passion of
William N. Valavanis

William N Valavanis

INTERNATIONAL BONSAI, ROCHESTER, NEW YORK USA

MMXIII

First published in the United States of America in 2013 by

International BONSAI
P. O. Box 23894 • Rochester, New York 14692 U. S. A.
www.internationalbonsai.com

Copyright © 2013 William N. Valavanis

All rights reserved. No part of this publication may be reproduced
in any manner whatsoever without permission in writing from
William N. Valavanis.

First Edition Printed in China by WKT Co. Ltd./Zebra IP

ISBN: 978-0-9884042-1-2
Library of Congress Control Number: 2013900487

Photography by Joseph L. Noga, Frank Grillo, Bill Kramer, Dean N. Valavanis, William N. Valavanis

Designed by Harvey B. Carapella
Color Separations by Joseph L. Noga
Editing and Proofreading by Louise R. Noga

Preface

This book is the result of my fifty year passion of studying and promoting classical bonsai art throughout the world. I feel sharing with others is important. Some consider classical bonsai art to be a static and old fashion form. However, I feel it is important to first understand the basics of this established and historical art and have spent my entire life in its promotion.

My bonsai in this book have been arranged according to how they are appreciated: for leaves, needles, flowers, fruit and finally as shohin bonsai. Some general care has been provided for each section as well as short interesting and instructive articles. Throughout the text valuable training and growing information is provided which has been based on my formal horticultural education, experience, research to develop new techniques and better plant care.

My extensive library of English and Japanese books and publications have been helpful in my research over the years and have contributed to my understanding of classical bonsai. Yuji Yoshimura's gift of his complete library added to the historical information which I share in this book, publications and many presentations.

Fifty years ago I was eleven years old and was beginning to learn bonsai, which I still am. Little did I know that a few of my primitive specimens would survive and develop into fine bonsai. Throughout the years I've had many cameras, decades before the onset of digital photography, and was always photographing my trees. I had no idea that some day those photos would actually come in helpful for others to learn. Tens of thousands of photographs and slides have been taken during the past fifty years, and unfortunately, a significant portion of those were lost in the fire which destroyed our home and office in 2009. They would have been helpful to fill voids in the developmental photos. Many were saved and have been used in this book for historical progression.

The bonsai in this book are the result of what I have accomplished during the past half century from untrained as well as a few established specimens. In Japan, masterpieces generally require more than one generation to develop and refine. We do not have that background in the United States. With the increasing popularity of bonsai, I'm looking forward to others for continuing and improving on my teaching and understanding of classical bonsai art.

The following mentors have influenced my bonsai life, philosophy and design: Yuji Yoshimura, Kyuzo Murata, Kakutaro Komuro, Mikio Oshima, Lynn Perry and Joseph Burke. A thirty year relationship with Yuji Yoshimura has opened my eyes and has guided me to continue his life's work in promoting classical bonsai art.

I'd like to thank my aunt, Lorraine Opitz, who started me out in my wonderful and joyous career that has covered a half century. I'm indebted to all my students and friends from around the world who have allowed me to assist them with their bonsai through the decades. I, too, learn from everyone and like to share my discoveries through my educational programs, teaching, magazine and publications. Working together, I believe, we can raise the awareness, popularity and quality of bonsai for future generations.

I'd like to thank Marc Arpag, Ron Maggio, Doug McDade, Christine Samuels, Harvey Carapella, Robert Blankfield and Joe Noga for allowing me to use photographs of their bonsai in this book to illustrate their beautiful bonsai. I'm proud of their work and have enjoyed assisting them during the past forty years.

I'd like to thank Ryan Bell (Japanbonsaipots.net) for his assistance in identifying many of the unusual bonsai containers that I've collected during the years to enhance the beauty of my bonsai. Archie Provan, retired professor of typography from Rochester Institute of Technology, has used his fine eye to made considerable suggestions to improve the subtle beauty and aesthetics of this book. Throughout the decades several photographers, listed on the facing page, have spent time capturing the beauty of my bonsai and have also taught me some techniques to improve my own photographic efforts.

Harvey Carapella, art director for International BONSAI, as always, has provided an interesting design for this book. His artistry and suggestions have improved the beauty of this book. Louise Noga, who proofreads for International BONSAI, has also done a magnificent job in making certain there are no errors and that my thoughts are clearly worded for everyone's understanding.

Joe Noga, in addition to being a fine bonsai artist, propagator and close friend, has contributed significantly to the final work you have in your hand. He has been photographing bonsai at exhibitions and my personal trees for many decades and his suggestions to refine the appearance of this book are invaluable. Professor Noga retired from Rochester Institute of Technology where he taught color reproduction for over thirty five years. After spending time photographing my bonsai he spent an additional four months adjusting the color of the images so they will reproduce perfectly. The four months he spent on this project directly followed the three months completing the photographs for the 3RD U. S. National Bonsai Exhibition Album. He now should have a well deserved break, but is working on photographs for the next issue of International BONSAI.

My family has supported and assisted me throughout the decades to share my understanding of classical bonsai art. I'd like to thank my wife Diane and sons Nicholas and Christopher for encouraging my passion and quest for additional bonsai knowledge. They have sacrificed so others could have the opportunity to learn and enjoy my bonsai art.

I believe it is important to provide sound and accurate information, based on experience and research, so others can enjoy and progress with their pursuit of growing and designing quality beautiful bonsai.

I have a special fondness for and am proud of my own original works of bonsai art. I hope all readers will find this book helpful to their understanding of classical bonsai, encourage experimentation and share their discoveries with others.

William. N. Valavanis
February 2013 – Rochester, New York

Table of Contents

Classical Bonsai Art–History & Aspects of Bonsai Styles 7
- *History & Informal Upright Style Design* 8
- *Cascade Style Design* 11
- *Formal Upright Style Design* 15
- *Slanting Style Design* 18
- *Other Bonsai Style Designs* 20

Deciduous Bonsai 25
- *The Culture & Training of Maple Bonsai* 26
- *Drastic Pruning Maple & Deciduous Bonsai* 28
- *Kiyo Hime Japanese Maple Profile* 32
- *Koto Hime Japanese Maple Profile* 39
- *Inarch Branch Grafting to Improve Design* 83
- *Improving Surface Root Display for Deciduous Species* 103
- *Bud Pinching Beech to Limit Growth* 136

Narrow Leaf Evergreen Bonsai 139
- *The Culture & Training of Narrow Leaf Evergreen Bonsai* 140
- *Moving Heavy Branches on Narrow Leaf Evergreen Bonsai* 141
- *Moving Heavy Branches on Larch Bonsai* 143
- *Origin of Dwarf Plant Cultivars* 160
- *Bending Narrow Leaf Evergreen Bonsai Trunks & Branches* 177
- *Approach Grafting New Foliage* 179

Flowering & Fruiting Bonsai 181
- *The Culture & Training of Flowering & Fruiting Bonsai* 182
- *Selecting Containers for Bonsai* 183

Shohin Bonsai 231
- *The Popularity of Shohin Bonsai* 232
- *The Matsudaira Shohin Bonsai Collection* 233

Bonsai Displays & Gardens 247
- *Alcove Bonsai Displays* 248
- *Bonsai Garden Views* 250
- *Profile* 252
- *Teaching & Sharing Bonsai Information & Techniques* 254
- *Publications* 255

Classical Bonsai Art
History & Aspects of Bonsai Styles

History & Informal Upright Style Design

Bonsai, a traditional art form of Japan, began its development in the 1600s to 1800s (Edo and Tokugawa Periods), but was refined and established during the 1800s to 1950s (Edo, Tokugawa, Meiji, Taisho and Showa Periods.) **Classical bonsai are highly refined, with a quiet feeling, which adhere to the standards established in 1829.**

The two books which significantly influenced classical bonsai were *The Mustard Seed Garden Manual of Painting* (Kaishiengaden) published from 1679 to 1701 and *Somoku Kinyo Shu* (A Colorful Collection Of Trees And Plants/Collection Of Tree Leaves) published in 1829.

Mustard Seed Garden Manual of Painting
The *Mustard Seed Garden Manual Of Painting*, originally published as a three volume series, was a manual to teach Chinese landscape painting. Students would see the printed brush stroke illustrations then copy and repeat the techniques until mastered. Once the strokes were perfected by repetitive practice, students had the basic background and freely created their own art. This style of teaching Chinese landscape painting is identical to teaching bonsai, first master the basics before attempting to create individualized personalized creations. Unfortunately, many attempt to skip the important basics.

An interesting and comprehensive article describing the *Mustard Seed Garden Manual of Painting* can be found in "The Vision Of The Literati In Literati Paintings," by Yoshiro Sakaibara, translated by Craig Risser published in the Winter/1981 issue of *International BONSAI* on page 10.

Somoku Kinyou Shu
The horticultural manual *Somoku Kinyo Shu* (A Colorful Collection Of Trees And Plants/Collection Of Tree Leaves), a two volume text, was published in Japan in 1829. This book features an illustration of a "classic bonsai pine" complete with twelve diagrams detailing "taboo" branches to avoid based on their shape, direction and form. The article states that if these branch formations are avoided a "perfect" classical bonsai can be created. The directions are strict and the text states that it is rare to create a perfect bonsai. The detailed formations are actually just good fundamental basic design principles as applied to living trees. *Somoku Kinyo Shu* is the first book to provide instruction on classical bonsai.

Yuji Yoshimura wrote the four part comprehensive article "Modern Bonsai- Development Of The Art Of Bonsai From A Historical Perspective in the 1991/NO. 3, 1991/NO. 4, 1992/NO. 1 and the 1992/NO. 2 issues of *International BONSAI*. In Part 2 1991/NO. 4 issue, additional information can be found on *Somoku Kinyou Shu*. The taboo branch formations have been expanded into the "Basic Principles For Neo-Classical Bonsai Designs" in Part 4 appearing in the 1992/NO. 2 issue.

Bonsai Classifications
Bonsai are classified using many criteria including shape of trunk, number of trunks, overall shape, method of planting, feeling, size, dead wood, focal point and others. The most prominent classification of bonsai is according to the shape of the trunk because that is the most important element of bonsai design.

Bonsai pioneer, author and publisher Norio Kobayashi (1889-1972) wrote numerous books and articles on bonsai. He is not related to the contemporary bonsai artist Kunio Kobayashi proprietor of the Shunka-en Bonsai Museum in Tokyo, Japan. Beginning in 1921 Norio Kobayashi published *Bonsai Magazine,* one of the most influential bonsai publications ever. This monthly magazine was published for 518 continuous issues and contains the complete history of modern bonsai in Japan as well as the Kokufu-ten Bonsai Exhibition. Mr. Kobayashi was one of the founders of the private Kokufu Bonsai Organization in 1934 who sponsored the Kokufu-ten Bonsai Exhibition until that organization reorganized as the Nippon Bonsai Association in 1965.

A magnificent bonsai photograph was featured on every cover of *Bonsai Magazine* which was surrounded by approximately twenty-five drawings or small photos of different bonsai styles. Throughout the decades of publication, *Bonsai Magazine* often changed the small photos or drawings, but usually maintaining the different styles named. It is interesting to see how the taste of Japanese bonsai remained rather consistent during the forty six years of publication.

Left–
Pine tree from the Mustard Seed Manual Of Painting *(1679-1701.)*

Below–
Classic bonsai pine from Somoku Kinyo Shu *(1829.) This was the first instructive illustration for designing a bonsai.*

Basic Classic Bonsai Styles

I will explain my understanding in detail of the fundamental elements of the basic styles of classical bonsai which I teach and use for creating bonsai. It is important to realize that like *The Mustard Seed Manual Of Painting*, the material presented in this series is just the beginning and one must understand, and perhaps create bonsai using these principles, before progressing to other advance or esoteric bonsai designs. The fundamental elements presented here are only the basics. **Not all beautiful classical bonsai have these elements.** To many artists this information may seem to be repetitive or strict. However, all beautiful classical bonsai have been influenced by the material presented in the book *Somoku Kinyo Shu,* published in 1829.

Respecting Age

The elements discussed here are the basics for an "idealized" bonsai usually created from cultivated plants (seedlings, cuttings and grafts). Other sources of bonsai material are trees collected from nature which may have an unusual trunk, branching or other interesting focal point which may not necessarily conform with the ideal. Despite this, these collected trees can make remarkable beautiful bonsai in a relatively short time period. But regardless of the origin and the time since propagation, an appearance of "age" is highly respected in classical bonsai and greatly enhances their quiet beauty. Like wine, the full measure of a bonsai can not be appreciated without allowing for time.

The appearance of age is in part a result of the design elements of the tree (root base, trunk line, proportion, branching and ramification) and the accumulated years of care. **Actual age and the appearance of age are not the same.** It is possible for a relatively young tree, well cared for, to show the subtle signs of "age" while an ancient tree with dynamic line, recently collected and trained, can betray a lack of refinement and care. The careful refinement of the design elements of a fine quality bonsai and the application of conscious, deliberate care will lead to a unified, congruent and undisturbed feeling of maturity and age. The subtle beauty and presence of a bonsai with these qualities can have a mesmerizing effect on its viewers and is the height of the art.

Dwarf Austrian pine, Pinus nigra *'Hornibrook,' trained as an informal upright style bonsai.*

Informal Upright Style

The informal upright style is the basic style of classical bonsai and probably the most popular worldwide. Many elements described here for informal upright style are also evident in other styles. The variations are mostly based on the trunk shape and movement.

Trunk Shape And Movement

An informal upright style bonsai is determined by examining the trunk line and movement. If a straight line is dropped from the terminal of an informal upright style bonsai, the end will usually fall near the base of the trunk. Trunk taper is important in all classical bonsai styles to suggest and sometimes exaggerate height and interest as well.

Trunk should display bark texture which is characteristic to the species. Also, it should not be scarred from poor pruning nor from wire not being removed at the correct time.

Silhouette

Like all styles of classical bonsai a triangular silhouette is prominent to provide visual stability to the design as well as to allow light to reach all branches. A triangular silhouette is also prominent when viewing the bonsai from the side. In fact, many fine quality bonsai are attractive when viewed from the back as well.

Crown

The top of the silhouette, or crown, is normally rounded to present the illusion of an aged tree, while younger trees are depicted with a pointed crown. Sometimes if the crown is pointed the branch tips are also pointed to create a harmonious impact. Likewise, if the crown is rounded, the branch tips are also rounded.

The branching is closer together in the crown and sometimes more dense than other regions. The top of a plant is more vigorous than lower areas and thus grows faster which requires more frequent trimming.

Generally branches are not positioned directly in front of the trunk. However, small branches are usually found all around the trunk in the crown region.

Lower Trunk And Surface Root Region

The trunk region below the first branch to the surface root area is perhaps most important because it attracts the eye and actually begins the trunk line. The trunk base of an informal upright style bonsai should display movement as well as taper. The surface roots radiating evenly around the trunk present stability to the design as well as adding interest especially if a root has a distinctive shape.

Branches

The branches of an informal upright style bonsai are artistically and asymmetrical arranged around the trunk. Branches are closer together toward the top of the tree and ideally taper from where they begin on the trunk extending to the branch tip.

Position the branches so they are on the outside curves of the trunk. Branches originating on the inside curves hide the negative space. Negative space creates interest and movement of the trunk.

Branches which are opposite each other on the same level are avoided because they present a static feeling and not a clear dynamic appearance. Sometimes one branch is allowed to lengthen to create a focal point which can also be created with dead wood on the trunk.

Containers

There is a wide range of container shapes and colors for informal upright bonsai. The selection of the perfect container depends first on the trunk shape and design of the bonsai. Next horticultural requirements are considered and finally the color of the clay body or glaze.

Generally any shape is suitable for informal upright bonsai. If the height is to be emphasized, select square, round or equal sided containers. If branching is to be highlighted chose a rectangular or oval container.

Personal preference is important when selecting the container and sometimes requires years to find and eventually afford. The quality and age of the bonsai must be respected for a good match.

Young bonsai are planted in newer containers than older specimens which should be growing in old or aged containers with patina.

Chinese quince, Pseudocydonia sinensis, *trained in the informal upright style with fine twig ramification distributed evenly throughout the entire silhouette.*

Daruma dwarf ezo spruce, Picea glehnii 'Yatsubusa Daruma', *although the trunk is upright the uneven lower branches add interest and direction to the bonsai design.*

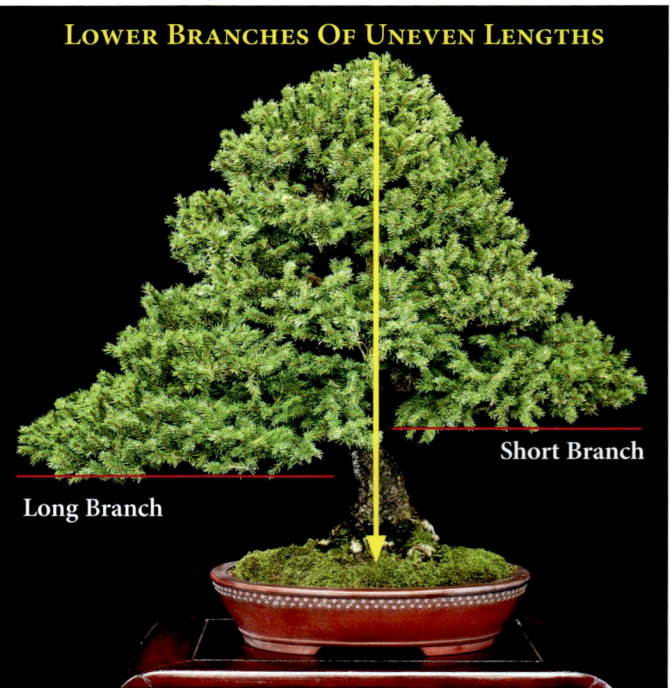

Cascade Style Design

The cascade style of classical bonsai features an "idealized" tree, perhaps struggling to grow upright on a steep cliff. Or an idealized image of a tree with a long low branch, either powerful or gentle, growing horizontal or downward.

Although this original concept may have originated from trees seen growing naturally in the wild, the form has been greatly stylized to reflect the combination of both art and nature. It is important to realize that collected specimens from the wild often do not conform to the idealized conception of bonsai and are individually designed to bring out the beauty of the specimen.

Cascade And Semi-cascade Styles
Historically two forms of cascade style have been established, cascade and semi-cascade. The difference being the length and tip of the cascading trunk. It is thought that the tip of the cascade style trunk falls below the feet of the container, while a semi-cascade trunk tip lies above that line.

Upon lengthy and logical discussions with Yuji Yoshimura, we discovered an interesting situation which does not make sense. What if a cascade style bonsai (with trunk tip below the foot of container) is simply transplanted, without changing the trunk angle, into a tall elegant container where the trunk tip now lies above the feet of the container? Does the cascade style bonsai suddenly become a semi-cascade? I don't think the style of a bonsai can be changed by simply selecting a new container. Therefore, the determining factors for distinguishing a cascade from a semi-cascade style bonsai must be altered.

The one permanent element of cascade style bonsai is the soil line level which does not change even if the tree is transplanted. If the overall mass of the "cascade" bonsai is above the soil line then the tree is a semi-cascade style. If the overall mass of the "cascade" bonsai is beneath the soil level line then the tree is a cascade style. This criterion makes sense, but is often difficult to determine.

Two-line Cascade And One-line Cascade Styles
Another major difference between "cascade" style bonsai, which is easily and more quickly perceived by the eye is some cascade bonsai have an upper trunk line and some do not, only having a single lower trunk line. I believe that the design differences between a one-line cascade and two-line cascade are more distinctive and easier to determine than a cascade and semi-cascade style. Therefore, I simply classify cascade style bonsai as a one-line cascade or a two-line cascade. One of the most important design elements for both one-line and two-line cascade styles is how the trunk rises from the soil. It should rise on an angle, not straight then bending over. A straight rising trunk is quite severe and the normal eye wants to continue looking upward, such as in the formal upright style. In fact, all styles of bonsai, except for formal upright and broom styles, look best if the trunk comes out of the soil on an angle, either slight or severe.

CASCADE OR SEMI-CASCADE STYLE?
Only the container has been changed, not the bonsai. Changing the container does not change the style.

Chinese wisteria, Wisteria sinensis, *trained as a two-line cascade style bonsai. Robert Blankfield Collection.*

One-line Cascade Style Design Elements

Since there is only a single line in the one-line cascade style it must be distinctive. In the two-line cascade style the eye looks upon both trunks. However, in the one-line cascade style the single trunk is the focal point and draws the viewer's attention. Soft and uninteresting curves are not as dynamic as sharp bends. Collected trees often have unique trunk lines and it is up to the bonsai artist to use them to the best advantage.

A simple trunk line movement, in a single direction presents a quiet feeling, while trunks suddenly growing back toward the trunk base are complicated. Classical bonsai usually display simple trunk lines and branching in harmony with containers.

The bottom of the trunk base must rise on an angle, not vertically from the soil line, especially for cascade styles, since it will attract the eye and create a still appearance. Ideally heavier surface roots on the side opposite of the trunk will present a feeling of stability.

One-line cascade style bonsai are not as common as two-line cascade style but are usually more dynamic and have tremendous movement which evokes responses from viewers.

Japanese black pine, Pinus thunbergii, *trained as a one-line cascade style bonsai. Harvey B. Carapella Collection.*

ELEMENTS FOR A CLASSICAL ONE-LINE CASCADE STYLE DESIGN

Straight Trunk Direction — Trunk rises on an angle from the soil

Apex — The sharp angle creates the dynamic focal point of the design

Tapering Trunk — Quick trunk taper is interesting and creates feeling of height

Branches — Delicate branching is in harmony with the elegant trunk

Silhouette — Overall asymmetrical silhouette creates a stable image

Trunk Line Direction — The simple trunk line has angular movement which is in harmony with the short straight branching

Two-line Cascade Style Design Elements

To achieve a simple unity with the design both the upper trunk line and lower trunk line should have movement in the same direction and rhythm. Both should lead the eye to the left or to the right. Trunks going in opposite directions are confusing and complicated.

Both the upper trunk line and lower trunk line should be of unequal lengths to avoid symmetrical balance. Either the upper line should be longer or dominant or the lower line should be longer. Avoid equal trunk lengths. Generally, the lower line is dominant. Ideally heavier surface roots on the opposite side of the trunk direction will present a feeling of stability. The upper trunk should be positioned at the outside of the trunk bend.

Ideally the first branch on the upper trunk should be above the point where the second trunk originates. If lower it will present a confusing feeling.

An overall triangular silhouette presents a stable design to the bonsai. The apex of the silhouette of the upper line is often past the container to present unity to the two-line movements.

Full moon Japanese maple, Acer japonicum, *trained as a two-line cascade style bonsai.*

Branches

Branches should ideally originate at the outside of the trunk bends so the beauty of the curves can be enjoyed. Negative space creates interest. If the main trunk presents a straight feeling, the branches should also to achieve unity. Likewise curved branches are better paired with curved trunks. The individual foliage pads should be triangular to allow light to reach all areas and present a stable design.

Containers

Tall rather than shallower containers are necessary to aesthetically and physically balance the bonsai for the cascade styles. Tall containers are elegant, but often difficult to effectively display. They look unattractive on tall cascade display tables and are better shown on flat boards or irregular thin cuts of wood slabs.

Containers which are semi-deep are more often used for cascade style bonsai than tall deep pots. In order to present a feeling of movement and stability to the bonsai, round, square and equal sided (hexagonal, octagonal and irregular round) container shapes are preferred. Long flowing trunks and branches beneath the feet of the containers present an elegant light feeling, while tall containers are aesthetically heavy.

In order to present a stable appearance for cascade style bonsai, round containers with three feet are arranged so two feet are visible from the front view. Positioning one foot under the long cascade trunk or branch is also a good idea for better stability.

It is important to securely tie cascade style bonsai to the growing tables to avoid mishaps. Tall cascade containers are not stable and are often tied to a vertical post to prevent movement. I've discovered that round containers like to "fly" in the wind and must be tied down using two pieces of string, rubber or wire, one on each side of the trunk. Long cascading trunks, especially evergreens are heavy and are easy to fall and break either the tree or the pot or even both.

Cascade style bonsai are also a bit more difficult to transport to workshops and exhibits. Often special supports must be constructed or sometimes the containers can be set into a bucket of sand to prevent movement and accidents.

Personal taste and your finances will guide you to select the most suitable container for your cascade style bonsai. Like other styles, evergreen species are often planted in unglazed quiet containers while flowering, fruiting and deciduous species are commonly seen in glazed containers. But the final choice is up to the artist.

Adding a cascade style bonsai to your collection will provide variety and will also become helpful when setting up an interesting display.

Selecting Containers for Cascade Style Bonsai

A round glazed container was selected to contrast with the intense new growth in spring. Glazed containers are often used for deciduous species. The round container shape harmonizes with the curved trunk lines.

Seigen Japanese maple, Acer palmatum 'Seigen,' trained as a two-line cascade style bonsai.

An unglazed brown hexagonal container was selected to present a quiet feeling. Unglazed containers are often used for evergreen species. The hexagonal container shape harmonizes with the straight trunk lines.

San Jose juniper, Juniperus chinensis 'San Jose,' trained as a one-line cascade style bonsai. Harvey B. Carapella Collection.

Formal Upright Style Design

The formal upright style is one of the most difficult classical bonsai to create and one of the most elegant styles to appreciate. The quiet, balanced and unimposing feeling of a lone tree growing up toward the sun is idealized in the formal upright style.

Trunk
Generally, trunk lines are the most important elements of classic bonsai and an important factor for the formal upright style. A formal upright bonsai should have a round, tapering trunk with an uninterrupted trunk line. The crown of the tree should be directly above the root base or slightly forward. Taper should begin with a heavy trunk base, which can be emphasized by strong well positioned surface roots, and continue up to the crown. Bark should be characteristic to the species and undamaged. Deciduous species usually have a smoother bark than evergreens which often have a rough bark texture like pines.

It is paramount to realize that there is no movement in a straight line and that design element is boring and does not show direction. Therefore, since the trunk has no movement the branches are the most important element of a formal upright bonsai.

Since there is no trunk movement, the trunk base should rise straight from the roots with no movement left to right or from the front to the back. The rise will lead the eye directly up the trunk in a straight line. For all other styles the base should not rise straight, but rather on an angle to compliment the trunk movement.

Dwarf Alberta spruce, Picea glauca 'Conica,' trained as a formal upright style bonsai with two trunks.

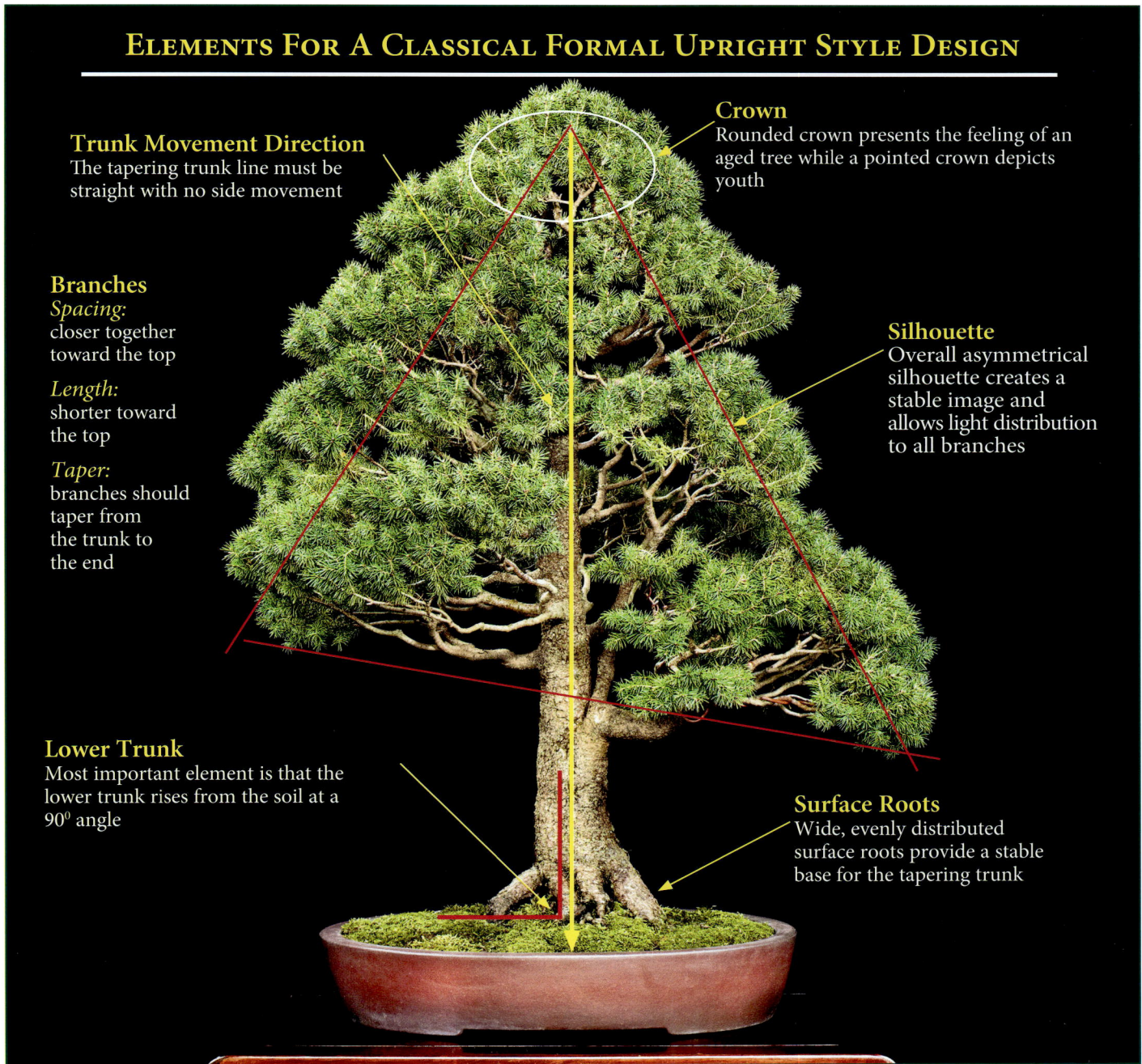

ELEMENTS FOR A CLASSICAL FORMAL UPRIGHT STYLE DESIGN

Trunk Movement Direction
The tapering trunk line must be straight with no side movement

Crown
Rounded crown presents the feeling of an aged tree while a pointed crown depicts youth

Branches
Spacing: closer together toward the top

Length: shorter toward the top

Taper: branches should taper from the trunk to the end

Silhouette
Overall asymmetrical silhouette creates a stable image and allows light distribution to all branches

Lower Trunk
Most important element is that the lower trunk rises from the soil at a 90° angle

Surface Roots
Wide, evenly distributed surface roots provide a stable base for the tapering trunk

Lower Trunk And Surface Root Region

All styles of classical bonsai the tree should begin with a well formed and balanced surface root region which adds stability to the design. The roots of a formal upright style bonsai should radiate all around the trunk, trying to avoid a heavy root pointing to the front. A heavy root on each side of the trunk, when viewed from the front, adds to the apparent thickness and taper. The roots should be firm to the soil with no airspaces below for best design of a formal upright bonsai. Bark on the surface roots, as well the trunk, present a feeling of antiquity.

Branches

There is trunk movement in all styles of classical bonsai except for the formal upright style. The broom style is derived from the formal upright style. Since there is no movement in a straight line, the entire design is dependent on the branches and their positioning on the trunk.

When appreciating any style of classic bonsai, except for formal upright style, the eye is attracted to two items, the trunk line movement and the branch arrangement. However, when studying a formal upright style classic bonsai the eye focuses to the branches and the silhouette of the composition.

It is easy to find plant material suitable for most styles of classic bonsai, but a bit more difficult to locate something for creating a formal upright style. Trees with straight trunks can be selected, but beyond that element, it is hard to find one with idealized branching. Selecting a specimen with branching in ideal locations is challenging, but remember, branches can be manipulated by pruning, carving and wiring. The branches should also be straight, with the lower ones slightly downward.

Branches should be of different thickness with the heavier on the bottom and the thinnest in the crown of the tree. The branch length is different for each as well. Back branches are shorter than the side branches. Opposite, crossing and overly thick branches are to be avoided when designing a formal upright style bonsai.

Consideration is also given to the spacing of the branches and should be closer together toward the top of the trunk. Branches should not be positioned on top of each other, but rather look like a staircase. The first branch is the longest, heaviest and extends from one side, slightly toward the front. It is located a bit higher than one-third of the height of the bonsai. With the branch lowered, the bottom will then be positioned at approximately one-third of the height which is pleasing.

Silhouette

The overall shape or silhouette of a formal upright bonsai is ideally an asymmetrical triangle. This shape allows for light to reach the lower branches and is also visually stable. Some artists prefer to create a symmetrical silhouette for their bonsai which can often be dynamic.

The silhouette, combined with branching, is what actually creates movement or direction of a classic formal upright style bonsai. A triangular silhouette with an even lower line presents a symmetrical balance. If the lower silhouette line is unequal an asymmetrical balance is created, plus movement and direction.

LOWER TRUNK AREA FOR FORMAL UPRIGHT STYLE

Heavy First Branch
Heavy first branch above heaviest surface roots

Surface Roots
Ideally should radiate all around trunk and are of different thickness and lengths

Lower Trunk
Most important element is that the lower trunk rises from the soil at a 90° angle

Containers And Positioning

Formal upright style can look pleasing in nearly any shape container. Asymmetrical shapes, rectangular and oval, are commonly used. Since the trunk shape is straight, branching is perhaps the most important factor when selecting the appropriate container for a formal upright style bonsai. Bonsai with severe branch angles, manicured compact foliage and pointed crowns look better in rectangular containers.

Bonsai with fuller branches, a rounded crown and horizontal branching are planted in oval containers, which are perhaps the best useful shape. Round, square or equal-sided containers are also used when the height of the formal upright trunk is to be emphasized, not the branches.

Positioning the trunk of a formal upright style bonsai in the container is essential to present a balanced appearance. The exact center of the container is not often used for asymmetrical containers, although some dynamic compositions are centered. Round, square and equal-sided shapes are usually positioned in the center because of the container symmetry.

The trunk of a formal upright style bonsai is usually positioned off the center point of an oval or rectangular shaped asymmetrical container. On which side the trunk is positioned depends whether a symmetrical or asymmetrical balanced appearance is desired.

Many artists position the tree in the container so the longest branch extends over the longest section of the container to present a symmetrically balanced feeling since the silhouette is equally positioned over most of the container. This positioning presents a stable, balanced feeling but does not create movement and direction to the entire composition. The straight trunk and balanced silhouette created by having the long branch over the longest part of the container is static. The overall mass or silhouette of the bonsai is equally positioned over the container and there is little negative area. Movement and direction are important when displaying bonsai and are used when positioning a bonsai in an exhibit or alcove.

However, one can also position a formal upright style bonsai in a container by considering the overall mass of the silhouette. Planting the tree with the longest branch on the shorter side of the container presents an asymmetrical balance and creates direction. Here the overall mass or silhouette of the bonsai is not positioned over the container.

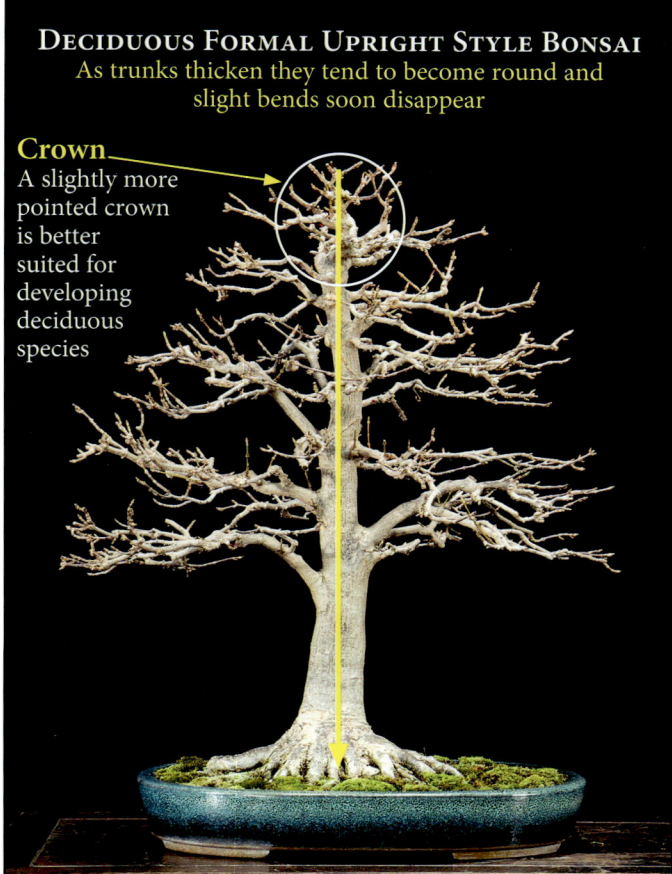

Trident maple, Acer buergerianum, – *formal upright style bonsai.*

The eye is attracted to heavy and darker areas and then usually moves to the lighter areas. Negative space is a key element in the artistic composition of bonsai and also display. Sculpture, painting and graphic arts all use negative space which can surround or include an object. This provides a rest for the eye and the opportunity for imagination and movement which provides interest. Breathing space is important when designing bonsai and also for positioning bonsai in containers.

Seiju elm, Ulmus parvifolia *'Seiju,' trained as a formal upright style bonsai from a field grown tree.*

Slanting Style Design

A slanting style classical bonsai is popular, perhaps because it appears different from the upright trees which are commonly grown and seen in nature. Perhaps people like tree forms which are unusual. Trees in nature are often knocked over by landslides from hills or mountains, yet the tree struggles to grow upright. Some trees growing on the sides of mountains or near water grow on a slant to receive additional sunlight. If the trunk leans over to a greater angle it is classified as a cascade style. The determining factor for a slanting style classic bonsai is the trunk angle which does not grow vertically. The actual trunk shape is not an element of the slanting style, only the angle at which it is growing.

Trunk
The trunk line of a classical bonsai begins at one point and moves to the other, ideally in one direction. The crown does not lie near the base of the roots. If a line is dropped straight down from the crown, it is not near the trunk base.

The trunk shape for a slanting style bonsai can be straight or curved with movement. Perhaps it will fold back on itself like many collected wild trees. Usually a simple slanting style bonsai will grow in one direction with movement back and forth to create a feeling of depth.

Taper is also important for a slanting style bonsai. It should be wide and stable at the bottom and gently taper to the crown.

RAF dwarf Scots pine, Pinus sylvestris 'R.A.F.,' trained as a formal upright style bonsai.

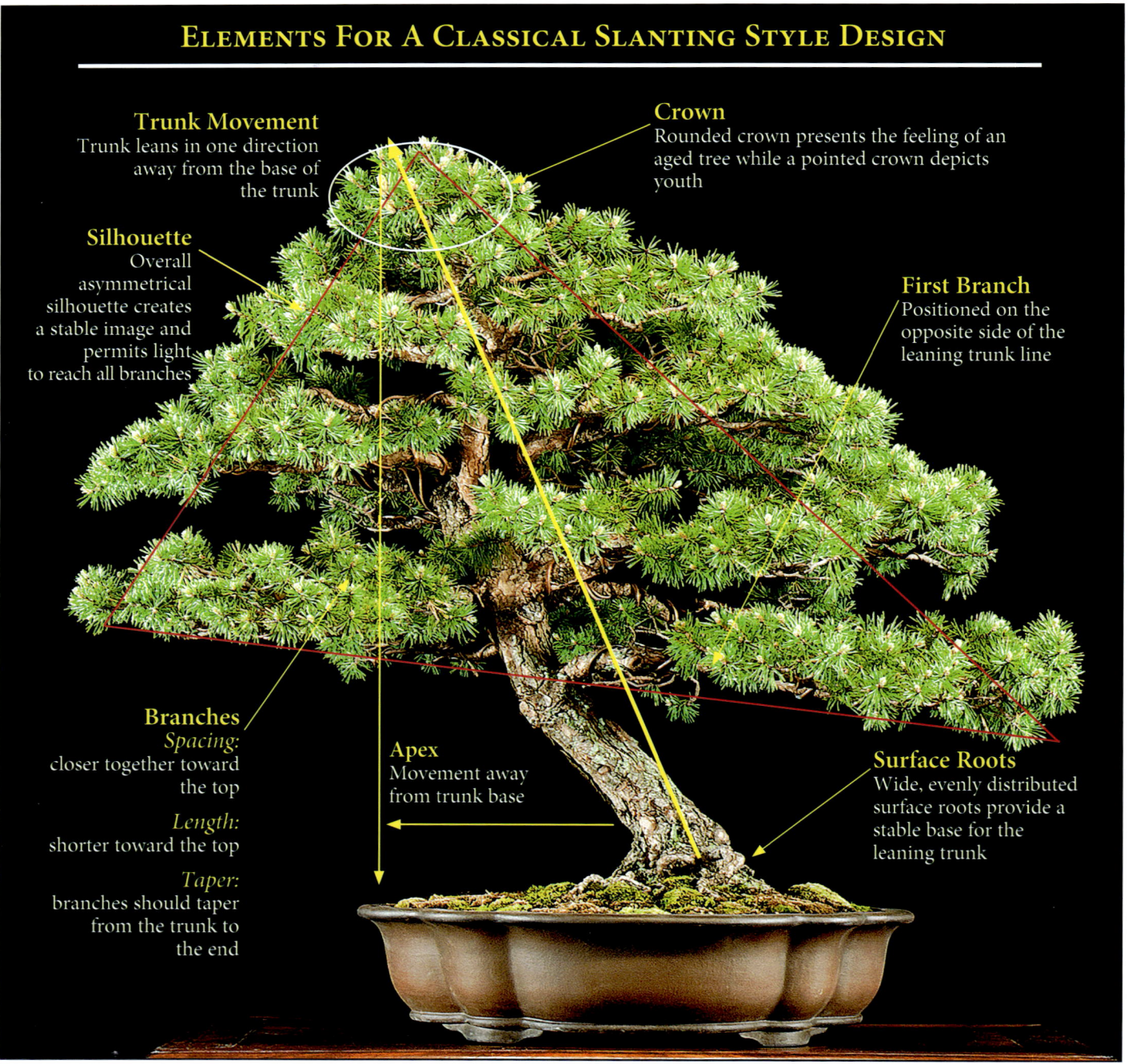

Elements For A Classical Slanting Style Design

Trunk Movement
Trunk leans in one direction away from the base of the trunk

Crown
Rounded crown presents the feeling of an aged tree while a pointed crown depicts youth

Silhouette
Overall asymmetrical silhouette creates a stable image and permits light to reach all branches

First Branch
Positioned on the opposite side of the leaning trunk line

Branches
Spacing: closer together toward the top
Length: shorter toward the top
Taper: branches should taper from the trunk to the end

Apex
Movement away from trunk base

Surface Roots
Wide, evenly distributed surface roots provide a stable base for the leaning trunk

Lower Trunk And Surface Root Region

The lower trunk and surface root region are an important part of every classic bonsai. The trunk rises from the soil level on an angle, not straight up. The trunk base should be heavy and provide the beginning of taper for the trunk. Ideally, surface roots should grow all around the trunk, however trees often exhibit heavier surface roots on the side opposite the slant of the trunk. This formation is to physically and aesthetically balance the leaning trunk. The surface roots on the slanting side of the trunk are often compressed, while those opposite the slanting style show tension to hold up the trunk.

Branches

Perhaps the most common characteristic of a classic slanting style bonsai is the position of the first branch. In a symmetrically balanced slanting style bonsai the first branch grows on the opposite side of the slanting trunk. Asymmetrically balanced slanting style bonsai have the longest branch on the same side of the slanting trunk, and it is balanced by heavy dense upper branches.

If the trunk shape has straight lines, the branches should also be straight for harmony. Likewise, trunks with curved lines look best with curved branches with movement. Bottom branches are angled downward while the upper branches reach toward the sunlight.

Branches can be better appreciated if they grow from the outer curves of the trunk all around the trunk. Those growing on the inside bends of the trunk cannot be fully seen and spoil the sensitive trunk line. If all the branches are on one side of the trunk, and of different lengths and thickness, the tree is considered to be a windswept style.

Like other styles of classical bonsai, branches should be of different lengths and thickness and should not be located above each other. Opposite, crossing and overly thick branches are to be avoided because they spoil the overall aesthetic impact.

Often a heavy lower branch is allowed to extend longer than normal to create a focal point. The directional movement of the focal point branch is balanced by heavier branches on the opposite side of the trunk.

Silhouette

The overall silhouette of a slanting style bonsai is triangular. Although triangular, the lower lines should not be on the same line and of unequal lengths. Remember, the lowest branch is usually the longest and heaviest, especially in a slanting style classic bonsai.

To present the feeling of an aged tree a rounded crown area is developed. A younger more vigorous tree is depicted by a pointed crown.

Containers And Positioning

Slanting style bonsai can be planted in any shape container. Asymmetrical shaped containers, oval and rectangular are commonly used with the trunk leaning over the longest section of the container. The trunk is not positioned with the longest low branch, (on the opposite side of the slanting trunk) over the longest section of the container. This design would lead your trunk line movement past the edge of the container and is not balanced. A comfortable balanced design is created by the trunk line leaning over the longest section of the container. This allows for a suggestive negative area opposite the first branch.

Long shallow containers are often used for slanting style bonsai with the trunk leaning over the narrow pot. This presents a balanced composition, but often the horizontal branches and long horizontal container line compete with each other because of strong parallel lines.

Round, square and equal-shaped containers, often deeper than shallow, are also commonly used for classic slanting style bonsai. These shaped containers emphasize the height of the tree and the leaning trunk past the edge of the container creates movement. The deeper containers visually balance the composition. Trunks are usually planted in the center of round, square and equal-sided containers for symmetry. To emphasize the height the trunk is sometimes planted a bit higher than normal.

It is a personal decision whether to emphasize the trunk and branch movement in a smaller square, round or equal-sided container or to balance the design in asymmetrical rectangular or oval container. Both designs are good and depend on the individual tree, container and preference of the bonsai artist.

Slanting style bonsai in round, square and equal-sided containers are sometimes unstable and top heavy which must be secured to the growing tables in your garden.

Crabapple, Malus sp., *trained in the slanting style.*

Washington hawthorn, Crataegus phaenopyrum, *in the slanting style.*

Other Bonsai Style Designs

The previous basic styles have been organized by the general trunk line. All bonsai are generally classified by the trunk line movement. However, there are other classical bonsai styles which are based on the: number of trunks, method of planting, feeling and size. Bonsai are also grouped by the size which is measured from the bottom of the trunk (not the rim of the container) to the apex for standing styles. Cascade style bonsai are measured from the apex to the lowest point of the design.

A few of the most popular styles and their characteristics are described here.

Bonsai Classification By The Number Of Trunks

Three Trunk Style Bonsai
All the trunks begin at the base of the largest and tallest trunk and are of different heights and thicknesses. The crown of each trunk reaches toward the sky and is not overshadowed by other branches. The heavy surface lower trunk and surface root region provide a stable base for the composition

Koto Hime Japanese maple, Acer palmatum, *'Koto Hime,' – three trunk style.*

Multiple Trunk Or Clump Style Bonsai
A single main trunk is the tallest, heaviest and creates the focal point for the bonsai composition. All other smaller trunks are shorter, thinner and have the same trunk movement as the main trunk for rhythm. The trunks are positioned unequally to provide interest to the composition.

Burning bush, Euonymus alatus, *– multiple trunk style.*

Bonsai Classification With Dead Wood Features

Dead Wood Style Bonsai
Collected trees are often trained for bonsai because of unique, unusual or fantastic dead wood areas. The dead wood features, whether being a section of trunk, branch or most of the composition, becomes a focal point because of the shape and whitish color which attracts the eye. Often the front is selected to highlight the dead wood areas. The dead wood areas are usually carved and shaped with power or hand tools to refine the shape. Cultivated trees can also be trained to feature dead wood areas to create a more dramatic design or reduce the trunk height by using special techniques to remove living bark and then carve and shape the wood. Dead wood areas are periodically treated to preserve the wood and prevent decay.

Eastern white cedar, Thuja occidentalis, *– driftwood style. Marc Arpag Collection.*

Bonsai Classification By Planting On Rocks

Rock Planting Style Bonsai
There are two methods of combining rocks with bonsai.

Root-over-rock Style Bonsai
Hard stones which do not disintegrate are used as the basis for a root-over-rock style bonsai. The roots growing over the rock are now serving the function of trunk and transport material up and down to the feeder roots planted in the soil. Roots which absorb water and nutrients are growing in the soil. The tree is never removed from the rock and is transplanted on a regular schedule for maintenance and health. Certain species such as Trident maples have characteristics of developing heavy roots which can easily clasp hard rocks.

Trident maple, Acer buergerianum, *– root-over-rock style. Harvey B. Carapella Collection.*

Clinging-to-a-rock Style Bonsai
All roots are contained in or on the rock. There are two types of clinging-to-a-rock style bonsai: vertical and horizontal plantings.

Horizontal Clinging-to-a-rock Style Bonsai
All the roots are contained in or on the rock. A sticky soil mixture is used for planting and wires are utilized to hold the bonsai to the rock. This type is often transplanted on a regular schedule for health and maintenance. Forest style bonsai are commonly planted on horizontal stones. Often natural or ceramic curved rocks are used to suggest a more natural feeling.

Dwarf Alberta spruce, Picea glauca, *'Conica,' – horizontal clinging-to-a rock style.*

Vertical Clinging-to-a-rock Style
Hard stones are selected for developing a clinging-to-a-rock style bonsai. Dwarf or slow growing species are often selected so they do not overgrow the balance of the tree and stone relationship. All the roots are contained in or on the rock. Trees are not planted in the interesting portions of the stone. A sticky soil mixture is used for planting and wires are utilized to hold the bonsai to the rock. Ground covers and small shrubs are added with moss to cover the planted areas of the rock to prevent erosion and help with maintaining moisture. Vertical clinging-to-a-rock style bonsai are rarely transplanted. This style requires additional over wintering protection during the winter and additional watering during the growing season. Clinging-to-a-rock style bonsai are often maintained in a shallow basin of sand or gravel to assist with moisture retention. They are formally displayed in water basins with moist sand or on flat boards or slabs of wood.

Kishu Sargent juniper, Juniperus chinensis *var.* sargentii *'Kishu Shimpaku,' – vertical clinging-to-a rock style.*

Bonsai Classification For Forests

There are two methods to create a forest or grove style bonsai: individual plants and root connected. Perspective can be suggested by creating a "distant view" or "near view" composition.

Forest Style– Individual Plants

Identical species are usually used to create a forest style bonsai from individual plants to present a quiet unified feeling. They are also easier to care for than forests of different species. Ideally unequal spacing of the trees is more interesting than trees evenly spaced in the container. The entire shallow container is not filled with trees to allow for important negative space. Young plants have fewer roots than larger more established specimens and are easier to plant closer together. Large trunk trees can create a powerful dynamic feeling of a near view forest image. Smaller trees usually express a more refined and quiet distant view forest image. The entire composition is not dissembled when transplanting. Sections of soil around the trees and on the bottom are removed, roots trimmed and fresh soil is added.

Chinese elm, Ulmus parvifolia, *– forest style from individual specimens.*

Forest Style– Root Connected Styles

Root connected style forest plantings are easier to maintain, but a bit more time consuming and difficult to create.

Forest Style Raft Style

The original main trunk can often be seen on the soil surface or just below. The trunk is in a straight line with no movement so depth is difficult to create. This style is rare, but the term is commonly used to describe any bonsai which is root connected. The original trunk will form adventitious roots and add vigor to the bonsai.

American larch, Larix laricina, *– raft style.*

Forest Style Sinuous Style

The original main trunk is on the soil surface or just below, and is often visible. Often branches are lowered and trained into individual upright trunks. The main horizontal trunk curves to the front and back to create perspective. This style is commonly mislabeled as a "raft style," but if the original trunk has movement it is a sinuous style. The trunk will form roots.

American larch, Larix laricina, *– sinuous style.*

Bonsai Classification By Feeling

A few bonsai styles are categorized by the feeling the form presents to the viewers because there is not a single common shape. Bonsai are often classified belonging in more than one style, with the most prominent characteristic being named first. Bonsai are usually named by the trunk shape, then the method of planting and finally by the feeling they present.

Literati Style

The literati style is an abstract style which does not have a single form but rather a light feeling. Trunks are generally thin and elegant and foliage is asymmetrically arranged. This whimsical style originated in China by scholars who painted to amuse themselves by creating images which pleased them, often inspired by nature. The form of a literati style bonsai is unique and depends on the sensitivity of the bonsai artist. The feeling of a literati style can extend to all other forms of bonsai. For example slanting, cascade or formal upright style bonsai describes the trunk shape, however the entire feeling can express the literati style. Therefore it is possible to have a cascade literati style bonsai. Cascade describes the trunk form, while literati describes the feeling of the entire aesthetic impact.

Sargent juniper, Juniperus chinensis *var.* sargentii 'Shimpaku,' – *literati style.*

Broom Style

The broom style suggests the form of a large deciduous tree with an abundance of delicate twigs as the focal point. Although many broom style bonsai have the branching originating in one area, many have the delicate branching up the entire trunk. There are several forms of broom style. This style is classified by feeling because many forms can suggest large trees with thin delicate twigs. Broom style bonsai are usually displayed in winter when the tree is dormant without leaves so the twigs and buds can be appreciated.

Japanese grey bark elm, Zelkova serrata, – *broom style.*

Windswept Style

The windswept style presents the image of a tree or trees which have been shaped or influence by blowing wind. Trunks can be single or multiple and usually all express the same feeling of being wind influenced. Often the branches are in a horizontal or slightly upward form. To enhance the naturalness of this style, the windswept style bonsai are planted in a curved rock or ceramic replica. The trunk or trunks combined with branches and twigs suggest being shaped by wind. A slanting style bonsai may express the feeling of being influenced by the wind, as may a formal upright style with a vertical trunk.

Mugho pine, Pinus mugho, – *windswept style.*

Deciduous Bonsai

The Culture & Training Of Maple Bonsai

Japanese maples are one of the easiest and rewarding group of plants for bonsai training. There are numerous different species as well as cultivars which are ideal because of their foliage, bark or growth habits.

Growing Environment
Some maple species and cultivars have a low tolerance for extremely cold soil temperatures in severe climates and may require protection in winter. Any extra work to provide winter protection to ensure healthy growth will be rewarded by beautiful and colorful spring growth emerging from the dormant buds. Maples being trained for bonsai in the garden, surrounded by insulating soil, are much more winter hardy than bonsai grown in containers which are surrounded by cold air.

Many maple cultivars have thin, delicate or dissected foliage which may easily burn under strong sunlight in hot weather and are best if provided some shade during the summer. Even in cold areas small specimens are best grown in semi-shade for the hottest parts of the summer.

Most maples are a fast growing species, such as Trident maple, and can be quickly created into pleasing bonsai with only a few years of training.

Watering
Maples do not like to grow in dry soil and love an abundance of free draining water. It is difficult to over water bonsai when grown with a free draining soil mixture. Although it is thought that watering in mid-day will burn maple foliage, I have not experienced that in my fifty year intense study of bonsai in New York, West Virginia and Illinois. It is important to thoroughly water any bonsai until water drains from the bottom of the container. When the water drains from the bottom of the container it draws in fresh air and is replaced. Thus, this watering technique improves the air circulation in the soil mass whenever the tree is watered.

Often developed maple bonsai have dense bushy crowns which shed water rather than allowing it to reach the soil. Therefore, it is often necessary to provide extra moisture when watering those bonsai, and may even necessitate watering during light rainfalls. I have been known to spot water using an umbrella for myself.

Fertilizing
Undeveloped maple bonsai are heavily fertilized with a high nitrogen content fertilizer throughout the growing season to promote vigorous healthy growth which can be used to shape and develop a basic bonsai design. In the upstate New York area I begin applying a water soluble fertilizer in May and conclude in October. In addition to a high nitrogen fertilizer applied weekly, a monthly feeding of organic fertilizer cakes is used to provide a steady release of slow release nutrients. This mixture of water soluble and organic cakes has produced excellent results as can be seen throughout this book.

It is thought that late summer or autumn applications of a nitrogen content fertilizer will promote vegetative growth which might be damaged with frost. However, this is not true if the bonsai has had a constant application of fertilizer throughout the growing season. In fact, the late summer or early autumn application of nitrogen fertilizer will help over wintering and provide an extra boost for spring growth. If the bonsai has not been regularly fertilized during the growing season it is not advised to fertilize after late summer. A sudden application of fertilizer applied in autumn may promote new tender growth, but the onset of shorter days usually prevents the onset of new growth.

After a basic bonsai shape has been created and established, the nitrogen fertilizer level is reduced to avoid strong vigorous heavy shoots which are unsightly and not desired, especially with a maple bonsai featuring fine delicate twigs. Heavy, strong and overly vigorous shoots will spoil the beauty which has taken years to develop. Only enough fertilizer should be applied to a developed maple bonsai to keep the specimens alive and healthy.

If the maple bonsai needs to be redesigned it would be faster to repot the specimen into a round shaped deeper container with a coarser soil size to encourage vigorous vegetative growth for a few seasons.

Soil And Transplanting
Undeveloped bonsai are grown and trained in a coarse size soil mix which provides more aeration and water drainage than a smaller size. Once the desired size and shape of a bonsai has been developed the soil is changed to a smaller size which

The spring growth of Japanese maples provide color in the bonsai garden.

Deciduous bonsai protected in a garage during the winter.

promotes slower growth and quickly develops fine delicate twigs. This advice is especially important for maples and other deciduous species.

Maple bonsai prefer a soil mix which has some organic matter for best future growth and development. I tend to think of the long range future, rather than a few years. Although maples, or most species, for that matter, will grow in any type of soil, as long as it drains, fine delicate twigs are best developed in a smaller granular size soil. It is best if some of the smaller size organic matter breaks down some because this reduces the air circulation and water drainage which helps create the fine delicate twig ramification.

Since the breakdown of the finer size organic soil reduces the water drainage it is important to carefully monitor transplanting. Undeveloped bonsai are transplanted more frequently than developed specimens because their root growth quickly fills the container. That is why a coarse soil size is used, to encourage fast growth.

Transplanting developing maple bonsai should be on a two to three year schedule, however, fast growing trees might be transplanted annually. Although root pruning disturbs growth, it also allows for quicker vigorous growth.

Developed bonsai must be kept healthy so they too must be transplanted, but not as often as developing specimens. Developed maple bonsai are not transplanted as often because fast, vigorous thick growth is not desired. Usually once ever three to five years should suffice for most developed maple bonsai. If the soil still drains well and the tree is healthy I generally do not transplant. However, should the water begin to slowly drain and health declines the bonsai is transplanted the following spring. The reduced transplanting intervals will promote short internodes and finer delicate twig ramification.

Although I have successfully transplanted most bonsai nearly any time of the year with extra aftercare, spring is the best time to transplant maple bonsai in the upstate New York area. Transplant deciduous bonsai in spring, as the new buds are swelling.

But I have learned the hard way, throughout the decades, that it is best to wait and not transplant when the buds swell because of late spring frosts which can damage new expanding buds and even kill, both pre-bonsai as well as developed masterpieces. I prefer to wait until the buds are opening to transplant and root prune. Even with the later transplanting time, careful monitoring of weather forecasts is necessary to avoid unexpected late spring frosts.

New Growth Maintenance Trimming
Developed maple bonsai must be continuously trimmed to maintain the developed form after it has been established. To develop fine delicate twig ramification with short internodal distances it is necessary to carefully pinch the center of each new opening bud before small leaves develop. This is a time consuming technique which cannot be accomplished at one time, but rather over the period of about one week. Each area of the tree grows at different rates and only the opening buds must be pinched. If a bud is missed it will lengthen and look out of place compared to the others with short internodes.

The top of the tree and branch tips tend to be the most vigorous and must first be pinched. Then a few days later the other branches behind these will be ready for pinching. Finally the inner buds will begin to open and must be pinched, and by that time the missed and slower buds in the other sections must be done.

The resulting foliage from this type of bud pinching will be small and compact. If correctly done, the tree will not produce any more shoots during the growing season. Therefore, the tree will maintain the size and shape. Since the bonsai will not produce additional branching for shaping this technique is not used for undeveloped trees.

While undeveloped maples are in training the new shoots are allowed to grow two to three internodes and then trimmed back to one or two. This allows the tree to slowly develop without getting out of control. Should a branch need lengthening or thickening it is not trimmed back as hard nor as often to allow for development.

Once the artist has decided that the maple bonsai has reached the development stage it is periodically defoliated to increase twig ramification, encourage smaller foliage and occasionally brighter autumn coloring.

Defoliating Maples
In late spring or early summer the developed bonsai is allowed to leaf out and is trimmed back to two or three nodes. It is important that the bonsai be properly fertilized to encourage healthy growth. One the new growth has expanded and matured the entire leaf blade is removed, allowing a bit of the petiole or leaf stalk to remain. If the entire petiole is removed the small desired bud in the leaf axil might be damaged. The remnants of the petiole will quickly wither and drop. After defoliation it is important to keep the maple bonsai in a full sun exposure to encourage small leaves. Once they form, if necessary, the bonsai can be placed in a semi shady area to protect from leaf burn. If the tree leafs out in the shade the leaves will not be quite as tiny as if it leafed out in a full sun exposure. It will not be necessary to normally water a newly defoliated bonsai because there are fewer roots to dry out.

If a developed maple bonsai was correctly bud pinched in early spring it is not necessary to defoliate.

Richard Marriott carefully removing the center tiny bud of each twig with a tweezers. This is an important technique to develop short internodes and small foliage. Since all the twigs do not grow at the same rate, several days are required to perform this time consuming technique.

Harvey Carapella washing the trunk and surface root region of his maple bonsai before transplanting. Liquid detergent is added to water for removing old bark, soil and moss which often grows on the bark. Washing the trunk also improves the air absorption of the trunk and lower surface root region.

Drastic Pruning Maple & Deciduous Species

Drastic pruning is a training technique for creating a bonsai or changing the size or design of an established specimen. Normally, drastic pruning is performed once in the development of a bonsai.

Drastic pruning removes large sections of trunk or branches. When drastic pruning to initially create a bonsai the plant is generally pruned back to the trunk or branches only, with no foliage remaining. Bonsai being redesigned often have the branches entirely removed.

Although any species can be drastically pruned maples, deciduous and broadleaf evergreens respond much quicker to this technique because the dormant or adventitious buds respond much quicker than narrow leaf evergreens. Broadleaf evergreen species which respond well to drastic pruning include: azalea, rhododendron, gardenia, fig and holly. However, Japanese andromeda, box and camellia do better with a minimum amount of foliage rather than complete removal. Many tropical or subtropical species are also usually drastically pruned leaving no foliage. It is dangerous, if not fatal, to drastic prune and remove all foliage for narrow leaf evergreen species for bonsai.

Deciduous species which respond quickly to drastic pruning for bonsai include: maple, elm, zelkova, apple, crabapple, serissa, flowering quince, Chinese quince, hornbeam, privet, pomegranate, bougainvillea and crape myrtle. Larch and dawn redwood are deciduous species which do not respond well to drastic pruning. Beech and cut leaf cultivars of Japanese maples are not as vigorous as other deciduous species and should be drastically pruned with caution.

I have successfully used the following drastic pruning and training techniques to create and develop many of the bonsai featured here for the past fifty years in Illinois, West Virginia and upstate New York.

Timing

Late winter to early spring is the best time to drastic prune deciduous species. Timing depends on local weather conditions and aftercare. The drastically pruned plants should not be allowed to freeze and should be kept in a frost-free location. It is best to drastically prune early in the season to allow a longer growing period. Later in spring may be the best in areas that are prevalent to late spring frosts. Plants can also be drastically pruned in late winter if kept in a greenhouse or other area until the danger of frost is over.

Ideally, the plants should have swelling buds and just beginning to grow. However, I have had excellent results with maples even when the new buds were lengthening.

Pruning Trunk, Branches And Roots

First decide on the height of the future bonsai and prune the trunk approximately one third below that area. I prefer to make a straight cut across the trunk, not diagonal. It can be altered later on when the new shoots have grown and the actual dieback area can be determined. Most specimens usually dieback a bit.

Carefully inspect the trunk for the surface roots, size, taper and shape, and then eliminate the defects. Proceed to the branches and first remove all heavy and wild branches which will not add to the future design. Often, all the branches are removed and are easily and quickly regrown.

Next the root system is pruned after the trunk and branches. This is the best opportunity to remove most of the roots. Since most, if not all the branches are removed, it is safe to remove

A field grown ten year old Trident maple grown in Florida before drastic pruning for bonsai in February 1993.

Trident maple after initial drastic pruning before cleaning and wound treatment. Continuing developmental photos for this bonsai on page 105.

quite a bit of the root system. I have, on many occasions pruned all the roots on maples and elms with good results. This may appear severe to beginners, but it is safe at this time of the year and stage of the future bonsai.

Sharp tools are important to make clean cuts. Remove any long and heavy roots, which prohibit the tree from standing on its own. A bow saw or reciprocating saw is used to make a single horizontal cut at the bottom of the trunk. Fine, fibrous roots are not needed at this time so do not be afraid to remove them. This type of drastic root pruning is hard on plants, but they quickly recover. I would rather "shock" the plant once in the beginning of its development rather than to "wait" a few years until it recovers. Often when one waits a few years to prune additional or heavy trunks, branches or roots, the shock kills the tree. I would rather have the plant die right away if it is not strong enough before investing many years in its training. This is an important lesson I have learned through the decades of actively developing classical bonsai, many of which are featured throughout this book.

Upon completion of removing any heavy trunk or branches each wound is carefully shaped. It is important that the wounds on deciduous species, especially maples are deep. If the wound is slightly depressed, the new callus tissue will extend beyond the trunk and look ugly. Also, make the wounds elliptical with

After drastic pruning a field grown Trident maple root system is washed to remove all the heavy old soil.

A reciprocating saw is often used to remove the bulk of the roots when drastic pruning and common transplanting using a sharp blade.

An abundance of vigorous new roots have grown in the first three years after potting using a coarse soil size.

A straight cut was initially made when shortening the height of the Trident maple. Note the section which died back and will now be removed.

Fine fibrous feeder root development after removing coarse soil.

Bottom view of the trunk showing a developing radial surface root system.

a sharp narrow end at both the top and bottom of the cut. This will stimulate a rapid callus formation more than a flat cut at the top of the wound. Concave pruners, chisels and power tools are often useful to make correct deep cuts after the initial wood has been removed. Sometimes Trident maples will quickly develop a thick ugly callus formation in late spring after pruning. This can be easily smoothed over in autumn when the growth is slower and it will develop better.

Next make sure the perimeter of the wound is clean without any jagged edges. A sharp knife works well here to avoid rough edges. Do not apply wound sealant until after the tree is washed and potted because it will become messy when moistened.

Cleaning The Trunk

After the tree is drastically pruned it is cleaned and washed before potting. Usually the trunk will be dirty and muddy. Use clean water with a little liquid detergent to wash the trunk and branches. Often I use Superthrive in the water solution. Begin with the top of the tree and wash the trunk working downward. Use a soft brush and gently remove all old flaky bark, lichen and other foreign matter to allow the dormant adventitious buds an easy access to the outside world where they can develop into future branches.

Seal large cuts with a tree wound dressing to prevent dessication of the wound and to promote quick callus formation.

Initial Potting

Use a deep training pot for the initial potting of the drastically pruned deciduous tree, even though it will fit into a much shallower container. Bulb pans or azalea pots are ideal, not shallow bonsai containers. Round training pots are better than those with sharp corners because it is easier for roots to grow without changing direction. Make sure there are sufficient drainage holes on the bottom.

A coarse soil mix is used for the initial potting to encourage vigorous vegetative growth. Particle size is very important. I use a soil mix which is approximately one-quarter to one-eighth inch in size. Make sure there is no dust in the soil to promote quick drainage. Soil mixes with large particle sizes have more air spaces which will promote rapid root development. A soil mix with small particle sizes promote fine roots and slow down the growth which are used for developed bonsai.

I prefer to position the trunk a little lower in the training pot than normal to provide an extra large watering space. The watering space helps to maintain moisture. After potting, use finely chopped long-fiber sphagnum moss on the surface of the mix to prevent soil from splashing on the trunk and to maintain a bit more moisture.

Wound Treatment

After potting the trunk apply a wound sealant to all wounds larger than one inch in diameter. I generally use Japanese "Cut Paste," but any sealant which keeps the wound from drying out will work. Quickly, new callus tissue will form and the cut paste will be pushed off. I have successfully promoted a smooth callus on four inch wounds of Trident maple in about ten growing seasons in the short growing season of upstate New York.

Aftercare

The newly potted trunk should be protected from late frosts. A daily misting of the trunk will assist in the formation of new adventitious bud development. Often I have taken a poly bag and loosely draped it over the top of the trunk, but not when the tree is in a full sun exposure.

The drastically pruned trunk should be carefully watched for dehydration and kept out of wind and strong sun until vigorous new growth begins and the tree recovers from the drastic

Trident maple four weeks after drastic pruning. All the new vigorous shoots are loosely wired into horizontal positions at an early age for best form.

pruning. Then the tree can be placed in a full sun exposure and do not worry about any leaf burn. The object now is to quickly establish the tree and train it for a future bonsai, not for display.

Training

Once new shoots begin to appear on the bare drastically pruned trunk apply a high nitrogen fertilizer once a week during the entire growing season. This will assist with the rapid development of new shoots which will form new branches in the future.

It is most important to begin training new shoots as soon as they grow to a length of approximately two to three inches. If they get too long they will be difficult to wire into horizontal positions because they are too brittle.

I wire all the new shoots, even though many will be eliminated as the bonsai develops. It is always prudent to have a few additional branches to help maintain vigorous vegetative growth. Extra branches can be easily eliminated in the future. When initially wiring these flexible shoots do not worry about crossing wire, and often it is loosely applied as it will only remain on the fast growing branches for a few weeks. If the wire is allowed to remain on the branch too long and bites into the bark, do not worry about it. These branches will quickly thicken and the wire scars will soon disappear. The main object here is to get the branches into horizontal positions.

The wire will remain on the branches for approximately three to four weeks before it is removed. During that time, other branches may have to be wired also. It is easier to unwrap the loose wire rather than to cut it off.

As the new shoots lengthen keep the top of the tree trimmed and allow the lower branches to lengthen. Since all the branches are the same age, they will be the same diameter. In order to provide interesting thicker branches on the lower levels, a few are allowed to lengthen more than the upper branches.

The future development of the drastically pruned deciduous tree depends on the future size and objectives. Generally the trees are allowed to grow vigorously all summer and are only trimmed once or twice a year. This helps to promote vigor and branch development.

Once the wounds on the trunk begin to cover over and the branches develop the tree is ready for potting into an oversized bonsai container. The length of time the tree remains in the training pot depends on the care and development, but generally about five years is sufficient. Once established in the bonsai container small twigs and foliage can be easily developed in a few short years.

Continuing developmental photos for this Trident maple bonsai No. 29 begins on page 112.

Trident maple after all the new shoots have been wired and bent into horizontal positions. Check the wire to prevent scaring of the bark. Allow all the branches to grow at this time to strengthen the tree. Final branch selection can be made at a later time.

A bushy tree has developed in only three months after drastic pruning. Keep the upper branches short to prevent over thickening. Allow one or two lower branches to lengthen to develop thicker branches on the bottom for variety.

Kiyo Hime Japanese Maple Profile

Acer palmatum 'Kiyo Hime'

Of the several dozen cultivars of Japanese maples which belong in the dwarf "yatsubusa" group, Kiyo Hime is one of the best for bonsai training. This unusual cultivar is a good example and quite representative of what the Japanese propagators group in the yatsubusa category. Yatsubusa cultivars generally have the following characteristics: multiple buds, short internodes, ability to root and grow adventitious buds from old wood, and sometimes small foliage and dwarf in plant character.

The specific Japanese terminology for these characteristics is "yatsubusa" and can be translated as "eight buds" or "cluster of eight buds." The term "dwarf" is commonly used to translate these specific characteristics, I often prefer to use the term yatsubusa because not all of the cultivars are dwarf.

"Witches' broom" is another term which is often used to translate yatsubusa. However, the Japanese term for witches' broom is "sekka" and many of the cultivars did not originate from witches' brooms, rather some from seed or bud mutations.

Another similar dwarf Japanese maple cultivar is Kashima also named Chiba, however this plant has an upright growth pattern while the branching of Kiyo Hime Japanese maple is strongly horizontal. Koto Hime Japanese maple is another popular cultivar for bonsai training in the yatsubusa grouping of maples.

Description

Kiyo Hime Japanese maple originated in Wakayama Prefecture in Japan. It is not certain if it was an unusual seedling or from a witches' broom, however, it is dwarf in plant character. A twenty year old garden tree, cutting grown, in Rochester, New York is now approximately three feet in height and six feet in width. Although it has experienced -19°F in a past winter and severe rabbit damage the previous season, it remains vigorous and healthy.

Generally Kiyo Hime Japanese maple develops a thick trunk in a short period of time. The branching is strongly horizontal with several layers of overlapping leaves. Another little known characteristic of yatsubusa cultivars which also applies to other species as well, is that they do not require high light intensity on the inner branches. Dwarf Alberta spruce, a bushy pyramidal dwarf conifer, will usually shed all its inner most foliage and small branches due to low light levels. Many of the dwarf yatsubusa cultivars including Kiyo Hime Japanese maple do not shed their inner foliage. Although the inner foliage persists, it is usually a bit larger than normal with a longer petiole.

Leaves of Kiyo Hime Japanese maple are a breathtaking sight especially in early spring with the intense rose-pink colored edges contrasting with the light green. The leaves later turn to a dark lustrous green, however, all new growth produced throughout the growing season will be rose-pink edged.

Another similar cultivar Murasaki Kiyo Hime, or Purple Kiyo Hime Japanese maple. This interesting cultivar, as the name indicates, leafs out purple rather than rose-pink. Many of the Japanese maple cultivars leaf out quite early in spring, including Kiyo Hime Japanese maple. Adequate frost protection must be given to plants which have leafed out early in spring to avoid frost damage to sensitive foliage.

Young plants of Kiyo Hime Japanese maple will grow quite vigorously for the first several years, and it is not uncommon for container grown three year old cuttings to produce new shoots up to twelve inches in length. As plants grow and mature they tend to produce numerous small delicate twigs and slow down in growth rate.

If older plants are drastically pruned in early spring vigorous new growth is initiated which develops abnormally large foliage. These large leaves reduce in size as additional small branches develop. The development of multiple fine branches assists in producing small foliage.

Propagation

Kiyo Hime Japanese maple can be successfully propagated from cuttings, grafts or air layering. Two to four inch terminal semi-softwood cuttings taken in May or June placed under mist can be expected to root in approximately six to eight weeks. Rooted cuttings will grow vigorously after the second year and require additional winter protection especially during the first winter.

Bonsai Training

Since the natural branch pattern characteristic of Kiyo Hime Japanese maple is horizontal, the most suitable style is cascade. However, any upright style can easily be created when training this versatile plant. Since the fine fibrous roots grow long and vigorously, they are also ideal for root-over-rock and clinging-to-a-rock styles.

If an unusual maple with small colorful foliage, dwarf horizontal growth and is easily trained for bonsai is desired, Kiyo Hime Japanese maple is an ideal choice.

Colorful spring new foliage of Kiyo Hime Japanese maple.

Brilliant autumn leaves of Kiyo Hime Japanese maple.

NO. 1 – KIYO HIME JAPANESE MAPLE

This Kiyo Hime Japanese maple was rooted in 1976 and was grown in a four inch training pot. In February 1978 it was sold as a two year old cutting to Donald P. Torppa in Charlotte, North Carolina during my annual Spring Southeast Lecture Tour. He planted it into a one gallon nursery pot using coarse one-half bonsai soil and one-half nursery mix.

The young Kiyo Hime dwarf Japanese maple was allowed to grow uninterrupted for two years. Several horizontal lower branches were encouraged to grow to increase the trunk diameter. The horizontal branching pattern is characteristic to this cultivar.

In 1980 the tree was transplanted into a two gallon pot and allowed to grow vigorously, except for taking a few cuttings to root. In 1981 during a private workshop with me, Mr. Torppa pruned, wired and shaped the initial design as an informal upright style with a long low branch. The following year the Kiyo Hime dwarf Japanese maple was transplanted into an appropriate bonsai container.

A few years later, during another private workshop session we discussed the design and changed the planting angle to create a cascade style bonsai. The bonsai container was again changed to compliment the design. Mr. Torppa was becoming more interested in developing a pine collection and in 1990 I purchased the bonsai from him and decided to refine the design.

The lower cascade trunk had been broken in an accident and in fact, was a bit too long for my taste. It was easily regrown and the point where it was broken became a bit unsightly but is gradually becoming less noticeable, especially during the growing season when the tree is in full leaf.

I transplanted the Kiyo hime Japanese maple bonsai into a larger and deeper bonsai container to quicken the development and refinement of the cascade trunk. In 1997 the bonsai was transplanted again into a fine quality Tokoname-ware Japanese container from the Reiho Kiln. I had three custom made containers made by Reiho for this bonsai, each of a different color. After considerable thought the blue glazed container was selected to contrast with the spring growth and autumn coloring.

The crown of this Kiyo Hime dwarf Japanese maple is a bit heavy and bushy now. Dwarf Japanese maple cultivars in the yatsubusa grouping have the characteristic of having weak crowns and suddenly dying after approximately twenty years. Since the bonsai was past the "overdue" date, I held off thinning out the crown waiting for it to happen naturally.

Throughout the decades I have learned that round containers like to "fly" and are not too stable, even when tied down to the outdoor tables or posts. Long cascading trunks are also vulnerable to accidents too. In 2005 one of my helpers accidentally broke the tip of the cascading trunk of the Kiyo Hime dwarf Japanese maple and shortened it considerably. A young new shoot is being trained to attempt to develop an elegant design again.

This Kiyo Hime Japanese maple was featured in the 2000/NO. 1 issue of *International BONSAI* and was one of the top 100 exhibited photographs in the 2000 JAL World Bonsai Contest in Kyoto, Japan. It was also displayed in the 2012 3RD U. S. National Bonsai Exhibition.

May 1999 – *Tiny red flowers can be seen at the tip of the cascading trunk among the bright new spring growth. Blue glazed Japanese container of Tokoname-ware from the Reiho Kiln.*

February 2000 – *The original branch break can be seen near the trunk. Nine years were needed to regrow and train the long cascading trunk which was broken again and kept shorter.*

April 2005 – *New shoots grew too fast to be pinched while emerging. They were allowed to lengthen then trimmed back to one or two nodes.*

March 2006 – *This is the best time to pinch the center of the new buds to develop small foliage and short internodal distances.*

July 2008 – An early spring prohibited bud pinching the bonsai in spring. The bonsai was not bud pinched but was trimmed back to two or three nodes to create a compact shape. However, the dense crown prohibits sunlight and air circulation and must be thinned out.

July 2008 – Large leaves and those hanging down were removed. After trimming back an occasional long new shoot and thinning out to allow light and air circulation to reach the central part of the bonsai, the tree presents a more compact and refined shape.

April 2009 – The new emerging buds were pinched in spring. This technique required daily pinching for a one week period. The foliage remained small throughout the remaining growing season.

April 2010 – The colorful new shoots contrast with the light blue glazed Japanese container of Tokoname-ware from the Yamaaki Kiln. The outer lip and cloud feet of the container are excellent for this design.

October 2010 – Small foliage developed as a result of dedicated spring bud pinching. The difference between the red/orange autumn foliage and the blue container are pleasing and typical of my taste for deciduous bonsai. The front of the container shows two feet which provides a stable feeling to the entire bonsai design.

November 2011 – During the growing season the bonsai fell off the table and the container shattered. Luckily, the cascade trunk was not damaged. I happen to have an unglazed grey Chinese container of the same size and design as the broken pot. However, the color is better suited for evergreens. The bonsai needs thinning, but looks great in winter.

NO. 1 – KIYO HIME JAPANESE MAPLE
Acer palmatum 'Kiyo Hime'

TOP TO BOTTOM 31 INCHES ▲ CONTAINER: CHINESE XIXING-WARE

JUNE 2012

WILLIAM N. VALAVANIS COLLECTION
ROCHESTER, NEW YORK

No. 2 – Kiyo Hime Japanese Maple

Kiyo Hime Japanese maples, like many of the yatsubusa cultivars are easy to root and also air layer. Many fine bonsai, especially smaller size specimens, were started from air layering. It is best to air layer maples in spring, just as the buds are opening for best results, although they can also be done during the growing season.

This bonsai was originally the top of a larger bonsai. In 1985 Joe Noga brought over one of his bonsai for a workshop. The height was too tall for the proportion of the trunk and branching so I suggested a reduction. Since the top branching was interesting, he allowed me to air layer his bonsai to create a new bonsai. The top of the bonsai easily rooted and developed into a three trunk small size bonsai. Unfortunately the original bonsai died a few years later.

The three trunk Kiyo Hime Japanese maple has excellent trunks and branching with the tallest trunk being the heaviest and the smallest trunk being the thinnest. This specimen has not been defoliated. Since it is a small size, it is bud pinched each spring to maintain the small foliage as well as to develop fine twigs with short internodes.

April 2005 – *Small leaves are beginning to develop by bud pinching in spring and will remain the same size during the growing season.*

November 2008 – *The red foliage provides a canopy for the surface roots.*

March 2009 – *Fine twig development by bud pinching.*

April 2009 – *The trunks have thickened but heights are the same.*

April 2010 – *All the leaves are uniformly small.*

NO. 2 – KIYO HIME JAPANESE MAPLE
Acer palmatum '**Kiyo Hime**'

HEIGHT 12 INCHES ▲ CONTAINER: ANTIQUE CHINESE

NOVEMBER 2010

WILLIAM N. VALAVANIS COLLECTION
ROCHESTER, NEW YORK

NO. 3 – KIYO HIME JAPANESE MAPLE

Growing Japanese maples from cuttings is enjoyable, rewarding but also a challenge. Although getting some cultivars to root is relatively easy, it is much more difficult to have them live beyond their first winter. In June 1976 when I had a good crop of Kiyo Hime Japanese maple cuttings, Yuji Yoshimura offered to over winter the young cuttings in his cool greenhouse. Those cuttings, with the extra first winter protection thrived and there are now several developed bonsai from the same crop.

This Kiyo Hime Japanese maple originated from the 1976 crop and was sold to a student years later only to be returned to me in a weak condition with many missing branches. The lower trunk and surface root system was impressive and it was worthwhile to remodel the design. The tree was transplanted into a large deep training pot from Korea for several years to first establish vigor so the shaping could be safely performed.

While establishing the new design suddenly both sides were attractive and could be considered as a front. So this bonsai is now being trained with two viewing sides, which comes in handy when setting up an exhibit. The trunk now over thirty years old is not producing new buds on the old wood so several branches were allowed to lengthen and were inarch grafted. They are now growing as one, but have not been separated yet.

November 2011 – *The dark blue container provides a heavy base for the bonsai design. White bark presents an aged appearance and begins to develop on Kiyo Hime Japanese maples after approximately twenty years when grown from cuttings in containers. Autumn foliage colors vary depending on the season and culture.*

NO. 3 – KIYO HIME JAPANESE MAPLE
Acer palmatum 'Kiyo Hime'

HEIGHT 18 INCHES ▲ CONTAINER: JAPANESE TOKONAME-WARE FROM THE SYUHO KILN

MAY 2010

WILLIAM N. VALAVANIS COLLECTION
ROCHESTER, NEW YORK

Koto Hime Japanese Maple Profile

Acer palmatum 'Koto Hime'

The Koto Hime Japanese maple is also in the dwarf or yatsubusa group of plants which are prized for bonsai training. This cultivar is best when trained as a shohin or small size bonsai because of the diminutive and tightly congested foliage.

Description

Koto Hime Japanese maple originated in Saitama Prefecture in Japan. The foliage is generally light green and is crinkled along the edges. Of all the maple cultivars Koto Hime Japanese maple has the smallest foliage. In spring the emerging foliage is colorful and appears as blossoms. The autumn color is not dependable for this cultivar, but the foliage generally becomes yellow before dropping in mid-autumn. Cultural practices and the current weather season determine the intensity of autumn coloring.

Another similar cultivar Goshiki Koto Hime Japanese maple has colorful new growth with white and pink leaves. The word "goshiki" in the horticultural world of Japan is used to denote plants with white, pink and green foliage. Although this cultivar is colorful in spring, I have discovered that the coloring does not last throughout the growing season and is not as vigorous as Koto Hime Japanese maple. Plants of most species which have variegated or colorful foliage are not as strong as the solid green leaf varieties.

The leaves of Koto Hime Japanese maple are closely spaced which means that there is an abundance of vegetative buds, even on old wood. This is an excellent characteristic for drastic pruning thick trunks and branches for developing or remodeling bonsai.

Most maples have an opposite leaf arrangement, but this cultivar often sports and produces a whorled arrangement. I have even seen branches form a fasciated or flattened shape, but it was not stable and worthwhile to propagate.

The most distinctive characteristic of Koto Hime Japanese maple is the extremely upright growth habit which sharply contrasts with Kiyo Hime Japanese maple which grows horizontally.

Propagation

Koto Hime Japanese maples are extremely easy to root as semi-softwood cuttings. Although cuttings can be taken anytime with good results, the ideal time for rooting is in late spring. Two to four inch terminal semi-softwood cuttings taken in May or placed under mist can be expected to root in approximately two to four weeks. Thick branches also root easy. Like other cultivars of Japanese maples, extra winter protection will produce healthy plants in spring.

Koto Hime Japanese maple can also be air layered with ease. Even large branches over one inch in diameter will root in approximately two months when taken in spring.

Bonsai Training

Since the natural characteristic of Koto Hime Japanese maple is upright the standing bonsai styles, (formal and informal upright and slanting) are the best forms to use. Any horizontal branching must be trained by wiring or pruning. Even if the branches are wired down, all future growth will remain upright.

Small size bonsai can be developed quicker than larger specimens, especially when air layering sections from large plants. Small specimens need small, neat foliage to be in proportion and this cultivar is perfect for that. The foliage is so small I have not found it necessary to defoliate to reduce the size. Small leaves often are deformed and do not resemble maple foliage.

Since the leaves are so tightly congested, it is necessary to thin out the buds each spring when they swell or as they are opening. This technique will eliminate many of the freely produced buds along thick old trunks and branches and give strength to the desired branches.

Should a branch get damaged, die or pruned, a new bud can easily and quickly be trained as a replacement. Allow the small replacement bud to extend without pinching to encourage the development.

Koto Hime Japanese maple has tiny emerald green foliage highly prized for small size bonsai.

Koto Hime Japanese Maple Development

NO. 4 – KOTO HIME JAPANESE MAPLE

This bonsai was started from a toothpick size cutting rooted in 1970 and was one of the original Koto Hime Japanese maples introduced into the United States. It has been completely container grown for the past forty two years. Perhaps large trunks can be developed faster in the ground, but this bonsai exhibits its age as well as a massive trunk.

It was grown in a small training pot and eventually ended up in a three gallon pot. I did not know the growth characteristic of this cultivar because it was unknown in our country so I just let it grow naturally as a stock plant for propagation. Eventually three strong trunks developed. Small branches and twigs rooted easily and I have rooted many thousands of cuttings from this stock plant and distributed them throughout the country. Probably most of the Koto Hime Japanese maple bonsai in the United States originated from this plant or one of its progeny.

I wanted to create a bonsai with the stock plant but did not want to waste the large branches. In April 1986 the top sections of the three trunks were air layered. Like cuttings of Koto Hime Japanese maple, they rooted quickly and the three air layers were removed in June 1986 and developed into excellent bonsai. All three are featured in this book and their original positions on the mother stock can be seen on the previous page.

Before the plant was air layered it was transplanted into a fine quality Japanese container of Tokoname-ware. Although the unglazed grey color is not my taste for maple bonsai, the container was empty and I wanted it planted in order to hasten its patina. Sometimes I plant annuals into containers, just so the pots receive daily water, occasional fertilizer and are exposed to the elements, which all add to the apparent age. Looking back now, twenty seven years later, perhaps the plant should not have been transplanted the same year as layering, but I did not know better and all three rooted well.

After removing the three rooted air layers the tree was drastically pruned back to encourage side branching. Each year the buds were thinned out and the branches were wired horizontally. In 1991 I found an unusual blue/green glazed container in Omiya Bonsai Village, which I felt was perfect for the developing bonsai. Later I discovered that it is a fine quality Japanese container of Tokoname-ware from the Koyo Kiln. The bonsai was transplanted in 1992 and began to get bushy, even though it continued to be used for cuttings.

Each spring before the leaves open the excess buds are rubbed off the trunk, and there are quite a number of them. Branches are occasionally wired now, but the continued pruning throughout the growing season is producing excellent coarse ramification of twigs. Koto Hime Japanese maple does not produce fine delicate twigs common to Japanese maples, yet has its own special beauty. New growth trimmed and is not allowed to lengthen because they will cause thick twigs.

Large Koto Hime Japanese maple bonsai are rare outside Japan and even there it is difficult to find well developed specimens. However, I did have the opportunity to see an excellent developed specimen displayed in the 2006 Taikan Ten Bonsai Exhibition in Kyoto, Japan. The bonsai was also multiple trunk style, planted in a shallow white container and I carefully studied the entire composition. I liked the container selection and found a similar pot for my bonsai. It was transplanted into a shallow white container March 2007 to emphasize the size of the magnificent massive trunk.

This Koto Hime Japanese maple bonsai was featured in the 1994/NO. 2 issue of *International BONSAI* and in *Fine Bonsai*. In 2002 it received the First Prize Award in the Midwest Bonsai Exhibit held in Chicago, Illinois. It was also displayed in the 2012 3RD U. S. National Bonsai Exhibition and was used as the logo.

It is both a challenge and delight to maintain this bonsai in the present shape because of strong apical dominance and numerous adventitious new shoots and I look forward to developing it further.

June 1986 – *After the three air layers were removed the plant was drastically pruned then transplanted into the new grey unglazed oval container. Cut paste was applied on the large wounds to speed up the callus formation.*

April 1992 – *The bonsai was transplanted in the unusual shaped blue/green glazed container. Notice how the wounds are covered with new bark. Horizontal branching is being formed by wiring the branches during the summer.*

April 1993 – *Continued pinching of the new shoots has resulted in additional branches. Note the different heights of each trunk.*

April 1999 – *The emerging buds are colorful and the trunk is beginning to thicken. New buds open and leaves will make the tree fuller.*

May 2003 – *Branches are periodically cut back to promote additional inner growth, even though there are an abundance of buds.*

March 2006 – *Fine branching can be appreciated without foliage. The bark is beginning to mature and develop the aged coloring.*

March 2007 – *The new shallow white container emphasizes the thickness of the powerful trunk.*

June 2007 – *The mature green foliage creates a different effect than in spring with the unfolding of colorful new buds.*

42

March 2010 – *Fine twigs have been developed by trimming the long new shoots. This bonsai is not bud pinched because they are too tiny and may be injured by tweezers. The colorful spring unfolding leaves presents a beautiful contrast with the aged white bark.*

October 2011 – *The foliage was burned during the hot summer and was unsightly so it was removed early to be photographed for the new book* Fine Bonsai.

March 2012 – *The irregular silhouette of the crown presents the feeling of an old mature tree growing in a park. Powerful surface roots anchor it to the ground below.*

no. 4 – Koto Hime Japanese Maple
Acer palmatum 'Koto Hime'

HEIGHT 22 INCHES ▲ CONTAINER: JAPANESE, TOKONAME-WARE FROM THE REIHO KILN

JUNE 2012

WILLIAM N. VALAVANIS COLLECTION
ROCHESTER, NEW YORK

No. 5 – Koto Hime Japanese Maple

This bonsai is the top air layered off the previous bonsai. Now, the trunk is just a bit larger than the parent tree and is developing into a great bonsai.

Air layering maples and deciduous species is not difficult and can be rewarding. Spring seems to be the ideal time for most species. Select the branch to be air layered carefully, if it has an interesting shape the development as a bonsai will be much quicker. Often the area below a forked branch works better than air layering on a straight branch section. Remove a ring of bark one and one half times the diameter of the branch to be air layered. Dust with a root inducing hormone, sometimes I moisten the peeled bark section with water first to ensure the rooting hormone sticks better. Actually, only the upper area of the wound will root, so that is the important area to apply the rooting hormone.

Next, wrap with clean long-fibered sphagnum moss. New Zealand and Chile produce the best and cleanest long-fibered sphagnum moss which orchid growers use. Wrap the moistened long-fibered sphagnum moss with a sheet of poly. Some use saran wrap, others aluminum foil. I prefer clear poly so the new root development can be watched. Tie both ends tightly to maintain moisture.

Watch for moisture loss and if the air layer looks dry, open the top tie and water. Then wait patiently, but it will not take long for maples air layered in spring. Soon thick white fleshy roots will appear through the clear poly. But, resist removing the air layer at this time. It is much safer to remove the poly wrapping and adding another thin layer of long-fibered sphagnum moss over the visible roots. In about one week an abundance of fine fibrous roots will quickly develop and it is safer to remove the air layer at this time. Remove a bit of the long-fibered sphagnum moss and plant in a training pot. Often the newly rooted plant must be tied to the training pot from the outside to prevent movement which will break the tender new roots. Do not tie the plant into the pot using wire in the soil as the roots are tender.

Although all three air layers from the parent Koto Hime Japanese maple rooted, this specimen had the best roots and they are carefully arranged each time the tree is transplanted. The heavy root base is quite impressive. In 2012 this bonsai was transplanted into the same unusual container the parent plant grew in for twenty years.

New vigorous roots appeared through the clear poly in two months. Do not remove, wrap with more long-fibered moss and wait one week for fine fibrous roots to develop.

June 1986 – *The parent plant was air layered in March and the newly rooted plants are ready for removal because of excellent root formation.*

Koto Hime No. 5

June 1986 – *After removal from the parent tree the air layer was planted into a training pot. Tie the newly rooted plant to prevent movement.*

May 1992 – *The trunks were allowed to lengthen to increase thickness, but they are too far apart from each other*

July 2003 – *The tops have been shortened to present a more compact shape. Suddenly the roots are beginning to thicken and develop.*

December 2005 – *Fine twigging is beginning to develop and can be appreciated during the winter when the bonsai is dormant.*

March 2010 – *The end of the right branch died and was removed. Colorful emerging new growth can be appreciated in early spring.*

March 2012 – *Transplanted into the new container the bonsai is now beginning to show the feeling of age.*

April 2012 – *The two side branches have been allowed to lengthen to present a broad triangular silhouette.*

NO. 5 – KOTO HIME JAPANESE MAPLE
Acer palmatum 'Koto Hime'

HEIGHT 23 INCHES ▲ CONTAINER: JAPANESE, TOKONAME-WARE FROM THE KOYO KILN

JUNE 2012

WILLIAM N. VALAVANIS COLLECTION
ROCHESTER, NEW YORK

no. 6 – Koto Hime Japanese Maple

This bonsai was the left trunk of the original Koto Hime Japanese maple which was air layered in March 1986. It was the tallest of the three air layers and grew well. Although it was the tallest, the trunk movement was not as dramatic as the other two specimens. It is developing nicely and the trunk is beginning to thicken quite a bit.

June 1986 – *After removing from the parent plant the new air layer was tied to the container. Chopped up long-fibered sphagnum moss was applied to the soil surface to maintain moisture and prevent soil from splashing onto the trunk.*

August 1992 – *The upright form of this bonsai has good spacing between the main branches. The surface root system is covered to encourage thick growth of the trunk base.*

May 2006 – *Fine twigging is beginning to develop and can be appreciated during the winter when the bonsai is dormant.*

June 2007 – *The end of the right branch died and was removed. Colorful emerging new growth can be appreciated in early spring.*

March 2009 – *The surface root system is developing and has been exposed. The branches are now ready for the annual spring trimming.*

April 2009 – *After trimming the bonsai was transplanted into a larger container. The trunk base has been buried to encourage larger development.*

NO. 6 – KOTO HIME JAPANESE MAPLE
Acer palmatum 'Koto Hime'

HEIGHT 13 INCHES ▲ CONTAINER: CHINESE XIXING-WARE

APRIL 2012

WILLIAM N. VALAVANIS COLLECTION
ROCHESTER, NEW YORK

no. 7 – Koto Hime Japanese Maple

Of the three air layers from the parent Koto Hime Japanese maple, this specimen was the smallest and had interesting movement to the trunk. I decided to keep it small and train for a future shohin bonsai. Unfortunately, it grew a little larger than anticipated, but is still a fine small size bonsai.

Like other bonsai the base of the trunk and surface root region were kept covered and buried deep to increase their thickness. In order to maintain the small size long shoots were not permitted to grow on this specimen. It was continuously pinched whenever new shoots appeared, but I stopped in early autumn before cold weather arrived. Like all deciduous bonsai it was trimmed back in early spring as the buds were opening.

This Koto Hime Japanese maple was the logo for the 2007 Shohin Bonsai Symposium.

June 1986 – *The entire removed trunk was allowed to grow undisturbed for about a year before it was drastically pruned for creating a shohin bonsai.*

August 1992 – *A deeper container was used to train the bonsai to encourage a heavy trunk. Long new shoots were not allowed to grow to maintain the small size and beauty.*

May 2006 – *A compact design with a heavy trunk has developed. In summer our dog ran into the bonsai and broke upper left branches.*

March 2007 – *Broken branches were replaced by an abundance of new shoots. This container is better suited for evergreen bonsai, not deciduous species.*

April 2007 – *After spring trimming it was transplanted into a finer glazed container better suited for the bonsai.*

June 2007 – *When this bonsai leafs out it presents a totally different feeling than when enjoyed in winter with the fine delicate twigs.*

NO. 7 – KOTO HIME JAPANESE MAPLE
Acer palmatum 'Koto Hime'

HEIGHT 10 INCHES ▲ CONTAINER: JAPANESE TOKONAME-WARE FROM THE KOYO KILN

OCTOBER 2012

WILLIAM N. VALAVANIS COLLECTION
ROCHESTER, NEW YORK

NO. 8 – KASHIMA JAPANESE MAPLE

Kashima Japanese maple, another yatsubusa dwarf cultivar, originated in Ibaraki Prefecture, Japan, approximately sixty years ago from an unusual seedling. This cultivar was widely propagated in Chiba Prefecture during the yatsubusa plant boom and is also known as Chiba Japanese maple. It was selected because of its dwarf plant character and small foliage. The leaves are more rounded, but about the same size as Kiyo Hime Japanese maple.

I taught a cutting seminar in June 1988 where students would learn the theory and techniques of how to propagate plants for bonsai. They would then make cuttings, put them in my mist house and return in August to pick up their newly rooted plants. Mildred Bruce from Pennsylvania was a regular in my courses, workshops, seminars and symposia. She rooted this Kashima Japanese maple in 1988 and took it home to grow. She brought it back to workshops several times and was growing it in a wooden box.

When she was not able to care for the tree in 2005 she gave me her plant. The base did not have well distributed surface roots. In spring I ground layered the Kashima Japanese maple to correct the problem.

A sharp chisel was used to scar the trunk base where new roots were desired, then dusted with rooting powder and long-fibered sphagnum moss was used to provide an environment conducive to producing new roots. The tree was left in the bonsai container and the soil level was raised using a well made from a plastic pot with the bottom removed.

An abundance of new surface roots developed in only two years. Later most of the original root system was removed and the tree was potted into the present container made in England.

This Kashima Japanese maple bonsai is quite vigorous and requires transplanting every two years and yearly leaf defoliation.

April 2007 – *The new surface roots are beginning to develop and are now being exposed to age. When buried, the roots will thicken, but the characteristic white bark does not develop unless exposed to the air.*

November 2008 – *Small leaves are encouraged by an annual complete defoliation, even in the years the tree is being transplanted. The roots are becoming vigorous.*

April 2009 – *Spring growth is beautiful and the leaves are tiny. The coloring quickly changes to a bright fresh green for the remaining season.*

March 2010 – *Two tapering trunks can be enjoyed after the annual trimming and thinning in spring.*

NO. 8 – KASHIMA JAPANESE MAPLE
Acer palmatum 'Kashima'

HEIGHT 26 INCHES ▲ CONTAINER: ENGLISH, GORDON DUFFETT

APRIL 2010

WILLIAM N. VALAVANIS COLLECTION
ROCHESTER, NEW YORK

No. 9 – Kashima Japanese Maple

I rooted a five inch cutting of Kashima Japanese maple in the summer of 1970 and grew it in a one gallon training pot for four years. After transplanting into a three gallon training pot the tree was used as a stock plant for fifteen years. Shallow bonsai containers were used for the next few years until 1994 when the tree was redesigned.

The excellent lower trunk and surface roots were developed by carefully spreading the roots of the young cutting and continuing every time the tree was transplanted.

The Kashima Japanese maple was developing nicely until a windstorm in the spring of 1994 blew it off the growing table and shattered the fine quality container and snapped nearly all the branches. Corin Tomlinson, Greenwood Gardens, Nottingham, England, was my apprentice at that time and this unfortunate accident allowed me the opportunity to teach him about recovering a damaged bonsai, drastic pruning and remodeling a bonsai.

All the branches were removed and the large wounds were carved and sealed. The tree was transplanted into a deep training pot with coarse soil and allowed to grow wild to help cover the wounds, grow new branches and hopefully look good again. The tree is now developing into a better form than the original bonsai and I look forward to the future.

This bonsai was featured on the cover of the 1983/NO. 2 issue of *International BONSAI* and also on the cover of the September/October issue of *Golden Statements*. It was used as the logo for the 1985 Maple Bonsai Symposium. In 1987 it was displayed in the Outstanding American Bonsai Exhibition held in Minneapolis, Minnesota.

November 1978 – *Two years after drastic pruning and establishing in a bonsai container, the basic branches have been selected for the design.*

June 1981 – *The tree was being used as a stock plant for cuttings and trimmed throughout the summer growing season.*

October 1982 – *The heavy right branch was cracked then lowered with a guy wire to improve the design. It was removed after a few months.*

February 1983 – *Small twigs are beginning to develop and the right branch needs additional lowering*

June 1985 – *The trunk still shows the color of a young tree and leaves have become smaller because of annual leaf defoliation began in 1983.*

June 1992 – *Transplanted in an English container by Gordon Duffett to enhance the appearance of age. The trunk base is beginning to thicken.*

July 1987 – *Displayed in the Outstanding American Bonsai Exhibition sponsored by the National Bonsai Foundation, Inc., at the International Bonsai Congress held in July 1987 in Minneapolis, Minnesota. The bonsai was defoliated before the exhibit and only had a few small leaves when I left Rochester, New York. The tree produced a lovely crop of small foliage in the car on the way across the country. Photo courtesy from* Outstanding American Bonsai *by Randy T. Clark and Peter Voynovich, Timber Press, 1989.*

April 1993 – The young fresh new leaves are evenly developed throughout the bonsai. The rounded crown is typical of large mature maple trees.

Spring 1994 – The well developed beautiful bonsai was blown off the growing table in a windstorm. All the branches were removed to redevelop a new design for the damaged bonsai. A complete photographic record of the drastic pruning and development was kept, but unfortunately was lost in our home fire. In 1985 Japanese bonsai master, Hiroshi Takeyama, who specializes in deciduous bonsai, saw the bonsai and commented on the strong branch on the left. He said it was too late to improve because of its size and position. Since the bonsai was already developed, and looking good, it was unthinkable to drastic prune for redevelopment. But, now I had an opportunity for improvement and began the journey.

June 2000 – Long vigorous branches developed in six years after the drastic pruning. The bonsai was only trimmed once a year.

March 2001 – Long shoots were only trimmed each spring. Old wood does not freely produce new shoots and some were needed in key locations.

March 2001 – Several branches were allowed to remain long for thread grafting to position branches where needed. A sharp drill bit is best for making a clean cut through the trunk.

Thread grafting is best performed in early spring before the buds open on deciduous species, but can also be done in early summer after defoliation. Maple wood is brittle, but usually the long new shoots are a bit more flexible. Drill a hold through the trunk where the new branch is desired, angle it downward since the future branch will probably be lowered. Make the hole slightly larger than the branch and carefully thread the branch through the hole being careful not to damage the buds. It is not necessary to scrape any bark, just pass the branch through the hole and seal both ends. I use Cut Paste with great results. Secure the branch with wire so it will not move. Often I loosely wire the new branch in a downward direction to help with future positioning. It is best to wait about two years before removing the old branch section going into the trunk.

May 2004 – Ten years after drastic pruning the new shoots from the previous season are colorful. This is the best season for trimming back last year's new shoots and for transplanting.

May 2004 – After pruning the branches and transplanting into a new container, by Gordon Duffett. The right branch was lowered with a guy wire for better design.

April 2007 – Branches were continually trimmed throughout the growing season, but need to be thinned out yearly.

April 2007 – After thinning out the branches to allow room for future growth. Notice the guy wire was removed after three years.

April 2007 – *After shortening the new branches and removing the guy wire the bonsai was potted into a deeper container to maintain the full canopy of leaves. Extra watering is often necessary during the summer because the dense foliage does not allow rain to reach the soil surface.*

August 2008 – *The bonsai is kept in the full sun, grew well and the trunk is beginning to thicken and become characteristically white. The leaf burn is not important at this time since the primary purpose is growth and development, not display.*

April 2010 – *In spring the bonsai was transplanted into a large finer quality container. Spring is a busy time here because of the many deciduous bonsai in my garden so there is not enough time to put green moss on the soil surface. I used ground up orchid grade long-fibered sphagnum moss from New Zealand or Chile for a soil covering. Green moss is planted before an exhibit or when time permits.*

    The twigs shown in the photo on the next page appear coarse because they are still young and the tree has not yet been bud pinched in spring. Although all the branches are the same age, each is of a different thickness which is accomplished by allowing a few branches to grow longer than others then pruned.

NO. 9 – KASHIMA JAPANESE MAPLE
Acer palmatum 'Kashima'

HEIGHT 27 INCHES ▲ CONTAINER: JAPANESE TOKONAME-WARE FROM THE REIHO KILN

OCTOBER 2012

WILLIAM N. VALAVANIS COLLECTION
ROCHESTER, NEW YORK

NO. 10 – JAPANESE MAPLE

Japanese maples are attractive all year around and this specimen has excellent twig ramification. This bonsai began as a young twenty five year old seedling grown in Japan and imported by John Kipp III in the late 1960s. In the mid 1950s he began studying with Yuji Yoshimura at the Brooklyn Botanic Garden and began Kawa Bonsai Company importing high quality Tokoname-ware containers from the Yamaaki Kiln. He issued yearly catalogs for his containers which were richly illustrated using his bonsai as samples. He did not sell bonsai, but accumulated and trained several hundred.

In March 1983 Mr. Kipp had an inventory reduction auction conducted by Keith B. Scott and sold nearly two hundred of his personal bonsai. Mr. Carapella attended the auction and purchased this Japanese maple for $100. Although the height is similar to the original size the trunk diameter has doubled. The impressive trunk and surface root region have been trained for many years with my guidance. Mr. Carapella can be seen washing the trunk and surface roots on page 27.

He has defoliated the Japanese maple several times during the past thirty years and has been training the bonsai to encourage fine twigs and small foliage. Now trained for nearly sixty years the lower trunk taper is superb and suggests a large mature tree growing in a park. It was displayed in the 2012 3RD U. S. National Bonsai Exhibition.

April 2006 – *Early spring brings a kaleidoscope of color to Japanese maples, the exact timing depends on the weather as can be seen in the photo also taken in April. The surface roots have been covered to present the environment for thickening.*

April 2009 – *Spring growth of Japanese maples varies according to weather, location of the bonsai and the individual specimen. The color of seedlings is different for each specimen, however, seedling from the same origin may have similar coloring.*

October 2010 – *Surface roots are exposed since they have thickened and actually have grown together. Note the color of this bonsai in autumn is similar to spring, but the leaves are larger and mature.*

May 2012 – *Fresh new growth which has been bud pinched remains small during the entire growing season. Since it now has developed fine twigs it is not defoliated during the summer.*

NO. 10 – JAPANESE MAPLE
Acer palmatum

HEIGHT 28 INCHES ▲ CONTAINER: CHINESE XIXING-WARE

OCTOBER 2012

HARVEY B. CARAPELLA COLLECTION
ROCHESTER, NEW YORK

NO. 11 – JAPANESE MAPLE

This Japanese maple was grown from a seed imported by H. Carl Young, Seiju-en Bonsai Garden, in Lodi, California in 1963. It was container grown until it was shipped to me in 1980 and I trained it for several years. In 1987 Brenta Sullivan liked this bonsai and it was added to her collection.

She trained the bonsai with my assistance. In 1993 Yuji Yoshimura conducted an advanced workshop in my studio and she brought her Japanese maple bonsai for critique. Mr. Yoshimura suggested that the height be reduced to make a shorter more powerful bonsai with a wide crown, typical of deciduous trees. After some thought she cut off the top and continued to train her bonsai. She gave me her bonsai in 2004 when she could no longer care for the tree.

A new container was selected for this Japanese maple in 2008 which was shallow and refined for the overall design of the bonsai. Small twigs are now being developed by bud pinching and an occasional leaf defoliation.

March 1980

The Japanese maple bonsai was potted directly into a bonsai container for training since it had a compact and fibrous root system.

November 1993 – *Yuji Yoshimura suggested that the top be reduced and after consultation with Brenta Sullivan, proceeded to cut it off. A few other branches in front were also pruned.*

May 1998– *Although the basic design has been established, the bonsai still requires years to grow fine twigs. The owner displayed her tree in the Upstate New York Bonsai Exhibition to share the beauty of a developing tree. The foliage of Japanese maples vary considerably. This tree grown from Japanese seed has small leaves which are especially attractive in spring and autumn.*

April 2008– *After transplanting into a deeper bonsai container, many twigs are beginning to develop but are not delicate and fine which present a coarse feeling. The removal of the top section of the trunk can clearly be seen. When the tree began to fill out the lowest left branch and another higher on the right were pruned to improve the design.*

April 2008– *After transplanting several of the branches needed to be lowered. Since the branches only needed to be lowered and not shaped, simple guy wires were used and removed in autumn before cutting in. The crown is beginning to develop and can be appreciated all year around.*

April 2010 – *The new growth was not bud pinched this year so short shoots would develop which could be leaf cut in June. The small hanging new foliage is especially attractive in spring. This vigorous and fast growing bonsai requires transplanting every two years.*

NO. 11 – JAPANESE MAPLE
Acer palmatum

HEIGHT 25 INCHES ▲ CONTAINER: CHINESE XIXING-WARE

OCTOBER 2012

WILLIAM N. VALAVANIS COLLECTION
ROCHESTER, NEW YORK

NO. 12 – JAPANESE RED MAPLE

There are numerous cultivars of Japanese maple which have been selected for colorful foliage. This Japanese red maple began as a young field grown grafted tree. Approximately thirty years ago Harvey Carapella purchased the landscape tree when it was four feet tall and five feet wide. After digging the tree he took it home and immediately bare rooted it to remove the old, heavy field soil.

First the height was established by drastic pruning the tree and all the branches were cut off. Finally the tree was planted in a deep training pot using coarse soil to promote quick, vigorous vegetative growth. He brought it to my workshops many times for advice.

Japanese red maple bonsai was displayed in the 2010 2ND U. S. National Bonsai Exhibition and received the Yoshi Bonsai Tool Award for the Finest Bonsai.

May 2000 – *This bonsai has not been completely defoliated, rather only the large leaves are removed. Note that the silhouette and size have been maintained while the trunk and branches have increased.*

NO. 12 – JAPANESE RED JAPANESE MAPLE
Acer palmatum 'Atropurpureum'

HEIGHT 30 INCHES ▲ CONTAINER: CHINESE XIXING-WARE

JUNE 2010

HARVEY B. CARAPELLA COLLECTION
ROCHESTER, NEW YORK

NO. 13 – JAPANESE MAPLE

In 1982 Joe Noga's son was helping pot seedlings and came across an unusual seedling with a "U" trunk formation. He showed me the seedling and I traded him one with a better shape for bonsai. At first it was potted into a Japanese style orchid pot with a wide drainage hole and tall feet. It was potted with the trunk growing out the drainage hole so the bottom of the trunk would not hit the table.

The bonsai grew and I shaped the trunk into an unusual form. Soon the tree outgrew the pot and Thomas Dimig was commissioned to create a new container for the Japanese maple bonsai. As the years went by he made two additional containers because the pot needed to be broken to remove the tree. In 2003 Dale Cochoy was commissioned to make a new container along with a removal stand to hold the pot.

I was getting bored with the odd, but elegant bonsai and returned it to Joe Noga in 2009. He commissioned Dale Cochoy to make a new pot and stand because the tree was growing large and David Knittle to design and make a suitable formal display table for the bonsai.

This bonsai was displayed in the 2012 3RD U. S. National Bonsai Exhibition where it received the Ho Yoku Award for the Finest Creative Western Formal Display.

June 2000 – *The second container for this bonsai was created by Thomas Dimig with long feet so the trunk would not touch the table.*

September 2005 – *The first container and stand made by Dale Cochoy.*

March 2012 – *The bonsai was transplanted into a new container by Dale Cochoy who also designed the ceramic stand which holds the tree.*

NO. 13 – JAPANESE MAPLE
Acer palmatum

TOP TO BOTTOM 14 INCHES ▲ CONTAINER: AMERICAN, DALE COCHOY

JUNE 2012

Joseph L. Noga Collection
Winterville, North Carolina

NO. 14 – SEIGEN JAPANESE MAPLE

This Seigen Japanese maple was created from a young grafted tree and has been completely container grown since the early 1970s. Rather than train it in the ground or a large training pot it was grown in a small bonsai container its entire life.

When the bonsai out grew the container it was transplanted into a slightly larger pot. This is the slow method to develop a bonsai, which is not popular today because people are in a hurry to grow bonsai. But, patience and respect for age is important in the development, appearance and appreciation of bonsai. When looking at this Seigen Japanese maple bonsai viewers can see the result of forty years of dedicated loving care which has gone into the creation.

Classical bonsai generally have one front which is the best viewing side. However, many fine bonsai can be appreciated from multiple sides, especially when planted in round containers.

This Seigen Japanese maple bonsai has two sides which are attractive. I dedicated about thirty years in growing and creating this bonsai from one side. Then one day the other side looked pleasing, and in fact had better surface roots. Having a bonsai which can be displayed from two sides comes in handy when setting up a display and a tree is needed in an area to go in a certain direction. Again, here is where round containers come in handy too.

Continued trimming produces many twigs and periodically the bonsai must be reduced in height and also thinned out to allow air circulation to reach the inner branches and for negative area. In 2011 this Seigen Japanese maple was thinned out and the bonsai looked a bit thin for one year, but looks better now that another year has passed. The beauty this bonsai presents in spring is appreciated by many.

May 2003 – *The bonsai was developed entirely in containers. In late spring the vivid red leaf coloring begins to fade to green for the summer.*

April 2005 – *The buds are evenly distributed throughout the tree and can be appreciated when the young emerging foliage opens in spring.*

April 2006 – *The new buds were not pinched this spring to allow the bonsai to rest for a season. Note the asymmetrical balance of the bonsai.*

May 2007 – *Suddenly a pointed crown developed and the right side silhouette looks flat which must be corrected.*

April 2010 – *The popular viewing side of the bonsai has been changed and displays a better root system. The basic structure of the trunk and branches can be appreciated before the reddish leaves open.*

November 2010 – *Seigen Japanese maple rarely puts on a colorful autumn display of leaves, but the weather and growing conditions were perfect to allow the bonsai to put on a show for viewers.*

March 2011 – *Before spring trimming to thin out the multiple thick twigs at the branch ends.*

March 2011 – *After spring trimming the branch ends are now displaying the fine delicate twigs.*

NO. 14 – SEIGEN JAPANESE MAPLE
Acer palmatum 'Seigen'

HEIGHT 27 INCHES ▲ CONTAINER: CHINESE XIXING-WARE

OCTOBER 2009

WILLIAM N. VALAVANIS COLLECTION
ROCHESTER, NEW YORK

NO. 15 – SEIGEN JAPANESE MAPLE

Seigen Japanese maple is well known in the bonsai community for having glowing spring growth color. The leaves are a bit smaller than the common Japanese maple and turn green a couple of weeks after leafing out. Autumn color is not reliable but sometimes becomes bright yellow.

This bonsai began as a young grafted plant which was field grown. After bare rooting the tree was directly planted into a large deep bonsai container because the branches were in good locations and I wanted to enjoy the spring growth color.

The long and elegant lower cascading trunk is the ideal length and proportion to the shorter upper trunk. The tree height was reduced a few years ago to improve the shape and to lower the height. It is important that the upper trunk line is in the same direction as the lower trunk line for unity.

As this Seigen Japanese maple develops in the future, additional branching will be encouraged and then fine twig development. The light blue container contrasts well with the intense red foliage and also looks attractive in summertime.

NO. 15 – SEIGEN JAPANESE MAPLE
Acer palmatum 'Seigen'

TOP TO BOTTOM 36 INCHES ▲ CONTAINER: JAPANESE TOKONAME-WARE FROM THE YAMAAKI KILN

APRIL 2008

WILLIAM N. VALAVANIS COLLECTION
ROCHESTER, NEW YORK

NO. 16 – SHARP'S PYGMY JAPANESE MAPLE

The Sharp's Pygmy Japanese maple is a common plant often used for ornamental landscape purposes. It was discovered by Oregon nurseryman, Jimmy Sharp in the early 1980s. The dwarf compact growth makes it ideal for bonsai training. The dark green leaf color holds up well through hot summers with little burning, even in shallow bonsai containers.

This Sharp's Pygmy Japanese maple bonsai was started from young container grown nursery stock propagated by a cutting in the late 1990s by Fred Stanzel. He trained the tree in a container and maintained the compact growth habit by trimming. Doug McDade obtained the bonsai after Fred Stanzel passed away in 2005 and has continued the development that was started over twenty years ago. He has brought the bonsai for several consultations during workshops for refinement.

A slightly larger fine quality container was selected for the bonsai because the trunk began to thicken as well as the surface roots. It has been displayed in many exhibitions in the Rochester, New York area.

October 2009 – *The glazed dark blue container has become too small for the bonsai with the large crown. The dark green color is maintained all during the growing season until autumn when it becomes fire red.*

NO. 16 – SHARP'S PYGMY JAPANESE MAPLE
Acer palmatum 'Sharp's Pygmy'

HEIGHT 22 INCHES ▲ CONTAINER: JAPANESE TOKONAME-WARE

OCTOBER 2010

DOUGLAS MCDADE COLLECTION
ROCHESTER, NEW YORK

No. 17 – Shishigashira Japanese Maple

Shishigashira Japanese maple is a cultivar which is commonly seen in rare plant nurseries and often in bonsai collections because of its compact growth and interesting foliage. Bonsai artists like the dark green, dense, curled leaves and dwarf growth.

This bonsai began as a young five year old grafted nursery stock obtained in 1969. It was potted directly into a small size shallow bonsai container and trained primarily by trimming. In the mid 1970s a section of copper training wire was allowed to remain on the trunk too long and cut into the trunk. The remnants of the wire scar can still be noticed just above the graft union.

By continued pinching and minimal wiring the bonsai began to fill out during the next twenty years. A larger and deeper container was used which quickly hastened the trunk and branch development. Suddenly the surface root region became beautiful after it was slightly covered during the developmental stage of training. Each year small attractive and interesting red flowers appear in May, often they form seed.

In 2011 several different containers were selected for this bonsai which resulted in a comprehensive article in the 2011/ NO. 3 issue of *International BONSAI*.

This Shishigashira Japanese maple was displayed in the 2010 2ND U. S. National Bonsai Exhibition and in the 2011 34TH Mid America Bonsai Exhibit in Chicago, Illinois where it received the First Place Award in the Professional Division.

April 1972 – *After potting in a shallow bonsai container.*

June 1981 – *The trunk was rotated to eliminate the ugly trunk curve.*

June 2000 – *Transplanting into a larger and deeper container the tree began to thicken. Notice the wire scars on the lower trunk.*

October 2003 – *A dark blue glazed container was selected to contrast with the orange foliage in autumn.*

April 2006 – *Small red flowers are produced each May and are followed by the characteristic winged maple seeds in autumn.*

May 2009 – *The leaf shape is different during the summer than in spring when the leaves are young and opening.*

April 2010 – *A white container was tried to emphasize the trunk color but after two months it was changed to a blue oval glazed pot.*

June 2010 – *The bonsai was transplanted into an American pot by Nick Lenz a few weeks prior to the 2010 2nd U. S. National Bonsai Exhibition.*

November 2010 – *Autumn often brings an abundance of bright coloring, but depends on the weather conditions and cultural practices.*

August 2011 – *A shallow wider white glazed container was used for this bonsai in August 2011 in preparation for display in the 2011 34th Mid America Bonsai Exhibit where it received the First Prize Award in the Professional Division. It was displayed with a summer theme hanging scroll and Japanese blood grass planted with a water pool suiseki in a round unglazed bonsai container.*

NO. 17 – SHISHIGASHIRA JAPANESE MAPLE
Acer palmatum 'Shishigashira'

HEIGHT 18 INCHES ▲ CONTAINER: JAPANESE, TOKONAME-WARE FROM THE REIHO KILN

AUGUST 2011

WILLIAM N. VALAVANIS COLLECTION
ROCHESTER, NEW YORK

No. 18 – Shishigashira Japanese Maple

Many years ago I admired one of Saburo Kato's masterpiece forest style Shishigashira Japanese maples and was looking for suitable material with no luck. It just so happened that David Easterbrook, former curator of the Bonsai & Penjing Collection at the Montreal Botanic was also looking for the same material because he also liked Mr. Kato's forest.

In 1977 David Easterbrook found three Shishigashira Japanese maples in a nursery with ugly graft unions. He wanted to use them to air layer branches for a future forest. It took him thirteen or fourteen years to successfully make suitable air layers and get them established for a forest. Since he kept his maples in a greenhouse, he air layered branches usually with more than one trunk in March. When rooted the new trees were removed in July and grown in training pots for a few years. He created the original forest in 2008 when he had sufficient similar material.

In August I visited Mr. Easterbrook's garden in Montreal, Canada, and immediately spotted the trees I was searching for, all arranged in a pleasing forest style bonsai. Although attractive there was one specimen in the center with a strange shaped trunk which did not quite have the rhythm as the others.

The Shishigashira Japanese maple forest was purchased in 2009. In March 2010 I rearranged the forest according to my own design principles which did not include the odd shaped specimen. That tree is now a single trunk bonsai.

September 2009 – *The bonsai arrived in Rochester without the container.*

March 2010 – *The forest was redesigned and potted into a new container.*

April 2012 – *The beautiful bright green spring growth of the bonsai is filled with red flowers.*

NO. 18 – SHISHIGASHIRA JAPANESE MAPLE
Acer palmatum 'Shishigashira'

HEIGHT 23 INCHES ▲ CONTAINER: JAPANESE, TOKONAME-WARE FROM THE REIHO KILN

OCTOBER 2010

WILLIAM N. VALAVANIS COLLECTION
ROCHESTER, NEW YORK

No. 19 – Deshojo Japanese Maple

Deshojo Japanese maple is a cultivar of the common Japanese maple selected for the intense crimson foliage of the emerging new growth in spring. After the colorful display of young leaves they begin changing to green and red before becoming all green for the remaining growing season. This cultivar is not a dwarf, but grows smaller than the common Japanese maple and makes a great ornamental garden specimen as well as an excellent bonsai for spring appreciation.

This Deshojo Japanese maple bonsai specimen was propagated from a rooted cutting over thirty five years ago, not a graft so there is not an ugly bulge in the trunk. It has been completely container grown and the young trunk was wired at an early age to provide movement for the future bonsai. The curves formed were not too smooth, but rather a bit severe because as the trunk thickens, gentle curves disappear.

The young plant was always grown in a bonsai training container since I got the young tree around 1995. The small bonsai containers have always been more shallow than deep to help develop the lower trunk and surface root region. The trunk base has grown, however the surface roots have formed like Seigen and Dissectum, heavy, but not webbing on the soil surface. Apparently the dwarf cultivars, such as Kashima, Kiyo Hime and Koto Hime easily develop a great wide surface root display. That is another good reason to grow and train the dwarf cultivars for bonsai.

This Deshojo Japanese maple makes a colorful focal point in my spring bonsai garden and also in bonsai displays when held during that time. Although the surface roots are not as vigorous as other maples, this cultivar is a pleasure for appreciation and bonsai training.

This bonsai received the 2011 John Naka Award in the Professional Division for a "bonsai designed from any plant material grown entirely in North America," which was sponsored by the American Bonsai Society.

April 2006 – *Allowing the left branch to grow a bit longer than normal has created movement to the silhouette.*

May 2007 – *When young, the bonsai was defoliated to encourage multiple branches and small leaves.*

April 2008 – *The bonsai appears to have a smaller silhouette before the foliage matures. In summer the entire tree becomes green.*

April 2009 – *The blue glazed oval container is better suited for this bonsai and contrasts well with the spring foliage.*

April 2010 – *In spring each emerging bud is pinched to maintain the size and shape of the bonsai.*

June 2010 – *In late spring the foliage becomes green and when mixed with red leaves presents a different feeling than in spring.*

NO. 19 – DESHOJO JAPANESE MAPLE
Acer palmatum 'Deshojo'

HEIGHT 28 INCHES ▲ CONTAINER: JAPANESE TOKONAME-WARE FROM THE KOYO KILN

MARCH 2012

WILLIAM N. VALAVANIS COLLECTION
ROCHESTER, NEW YORK

No. 20 – Cutleaf Japanese Red Maple

There are approximately fifty different cultivars of Japanese maples with cut or dissected foliage. They vary in leaf color, size, shape and growth habit. Cultivars with green foliage are more vigorous than ones with red or variegated leaves.

This specimen was trained from a grafted field grown nursery stock which was purchased in April 1985 balled and burlapped. At that time the tree was bare rooted and potted in a large unglazed clay flower pot for training. The soil was coarse including chicken grit to promote quick drainage and fast growth.

Approximately five years later the bonsai was potted into a rectangular blue glazed container and was trained in a classic slanting style. In 2008 it was potted into a shallow round container to emphasize the delicate well tapered trunk line and short branches to provide a light and airy feeling.

This Cutleaf Japanese red maple is being trained in the literati style and is attractive in both spring and autumn when it consistently provides viewers with striking orange red foliage. It was displayed in the 2010 2ⁿᴅ U. S. National Bonsai Exhibition.

May 2004 – *The lovely weeping branches with bright red fine delicate leaves presented a colorful impact in several bonsai exhibitions.*

April 2008 – *The tree was cut back to encourage additional branching in the inner sections of the tree. The base surface roots are developing.*

May 2010 – *Round containers are best used to emphasize the height and reduce the width of branches.*

May 2010 – *This bonsai is pleasing from many sides and the surface roots are well distributed.*

NO. 20 – CUTLEAF JAPANESE RED MAPLE
Acer palmatum 'Dissectum Atropurpureum'

HEIGHT 33 INCHES ▲ CONTAINER: CHINESE

JUNE 2010

WILLIAM N. VALAVANIS COLLECTION
ROCHESTER, NEW YORK

No. 21 – Rough Bark Japanese Maple

The Rough bark Japanese maple is a cultivar which has been selected for its unique rough bark which forms in small sections. Other rough bark varieties tend to have short lasting bark, but this cultivar has long lasting hard bark. The bark and coarse branching do not present a delicate appearance and is quite a bit different than the common Japanese maple.

Spring growth is tinged with red, while in autumn the reliable coloring can vary from yellow to orange and red which make a focal point in my garden. The leaves are the size of the common Japanese maple and is a fast grower.

In 1975 I rooted several cuttings of this choice cultivar. Of the original crop only two now remain, the bonsai featured here and one which was planted in my garden. This bonsai was completely container grown in smaller bonsai containers. The other specimen was grown in a five gallon pot and was allowed to grow large for a garden tree.

The large tree was planted into my garden when it was approximately five feet tall twenty five years ago and allowed to grow to a large size for cutting propagation. It now produces many seedlings, but it is not known if they will develop rough bark. Since the tree was propagated from a cutting it is genetically uniform and a surface root six feet away from the fourteen inch trunk base also has rough bark. I did not allow the bonsai to grow long shoots because that would destroy the developing twigs, and only took cuttings from the bonsai.

Many years ago a few of the upper branches and terminal was broken in an accident, but vigorous growth has replaced the missing limbs and actually helped the design by reducing the height.

Unfortunately the old rough bark does not easily produce new buds so it has been necessary to inarch branches to replace missing branches or add branches where necessary. The branch grafts are best made in spring before the buds open so the branch tips can be easily pushed through the trunk.

November 2003 – *The terminal and several upper branches were broken in an accident and are beginning to be replaced.*

July 2004 – *New twigs are growing strong in the crown of the bonsai. The bright green summer growth contrasts with the blue container.*

April 2005 – *An unglazed grey oval container was selected which is better for the design, but not for the autumn color.*

November 2006 – *The golden autumn foliage is pleasing but does not contrast with the unglazed container which is better suited for evergreens.*

November 2010 – A new blue glazed oval container, of the same design as the previous pot, was used for this bonsai.

November 2010 – An impressive lower trunk and surface root system has developed during the past thirty eight years.

Inarch Branch Grafting To Improve Bonsai Design

Use a sharp wood drill bit to make a hole through the trunk where the new branch is desired. I prefer to begin the hole where the new branch is desired then drill through to the other side. Hold the trunk on the other side of the drill entrance.

Select a long slender branch to be thread grafted. It may be easier to wire the base of the long branch so it does not snap when bending through the hole. Pull the branch through the hole until a bud is positioned at the desired position.

Deciduous species are best grafted in spring while the buds are still closed so they can be passed through the hole. Be sure not to injure the tender buds. Wire the end branch to keep it from moving and slightly bend it down. Do not injure the bud. Inarch grafting can also be done in summer after defoliation.

It is often best to grow the new branch from the bud at the base of the hole because closer branching can be developed. Finally, seal both ends to prevent movement and retain moisture. I use Cut Paste. It is not necessary to scrape the threaded branch. Wait one or two years before removing the branch leading into the trunk.

NO. 21 – ROUGH BARK JAPANESE MAPLE
Acer palmatum 'Arakawa'

HEIGHT 29 INCHES ▲ CONTAINER: CHINESE XIXING-WARE

NOVEMBER 2012

WILLIAM N. VALAVANIS COLLECTION
ROCHESTER, NEW YORK

No. 22 – Full-Moon Maple

The Full-Moon maple is not often seen trained as bonsai. Native to Japan it has seven to thirteen leaf lobes, while the common Japanese maple has five to seven leaf lobes. The cultivar, Golden full-moon maple, is commonly grown in the garden landscape and trained for bonsai as well.

This species has rather large size leaves and is not suitable for small size shohin bonsai. Since the foliage is large I trained the bonsai so the foliage would be in proportion to the Full-moon maple bonsai.

I purchased this specimen from Yuji Yoshimura for $1.50 as a ten year old seedling in a two gallon pot in 1975. He had made one cut on the trunk and the tree began to branch out at that point. The tree was transplanted into several different containers for the next twenty five years.

Since the foliage is large the bonsai was defoliated several times in the 1980s. The vigor has slowed down for this mature specimen and does not currently respond well to defoliation. I continued to grow and train this bonsai with the original front which was selected in 1975. In 1995 during a workshop, I turned the tree around and discovered another front for this bonsai. I was not looking for a new front, the new front just jumped out at me. The changed front has more trunk movement and better surface roots which had developed during the past twenty years.

Since the new front was more informal and elegant than the original form a new shallower oval container was selected. In 1985 the bonsai grew so much that a larger container was necessary. Since I liked the oval container it was in, a larger pot of the same design and color was ordered from Japan. Now the bonsai is becoming too heavy for me to lift and requires two people for moving.

When studying the photographs I found the increase in the massive trunk thickness amazing, especially since the bonsai has never been in the ground, nor drastically pruned, except for the initial cut by Yuji Yoshimura.

A photograph of this bonsai was featured on the cover of Dorothy S. Young's book *Bonsai: It's Art and Technique*. It was also featured on the covers of the 1993/NO. 3 and 2000/NO. 2 issues of *International BONSAI*. This Full-moon maple was one of the top 100 exhibited photographs in the 1999 JAL World Bonsai Contest in Kyoto, Japan.

October 1980 – *The first potting for this bonsai was an unglazed deep oval container.*

May 1981 – *Since the trunk was straight and had little movement a white glazed rectangular container was selected for the bonsai.*

October 1982 – *The autumn coloring for Full moon maple bonsai is usually outstanding, especially after defoliation.*

March 1983 – *The basic trunk structure can be studied during winter.*

June 1984 – *Foliage during the summer adds mass to the silhouette.*

May 1995 – *A larger and deeper container was selected for balance.*

October 1985 – *Smaller foliage developed after leaf defoliation.*

May 1999 – *The bonsai has an elegant form in the new container.*

May 2000 – *Mature foliage is trimmed after elongation in early summer.*

April 2006 – *The new buds must be pinched when opening in spring to maintain the size of the bonsai.*

May 2008 – *Suddenly the trunk is beginning to thicken. A branch on the right is being lowered.*

NO. 22 – FULL-MOON MAPLE
Acer japonicum

HEIGHT 36 INCHES ▲ CONTAINER: JAPANESE TOKONAME-WARE FROM THE SUISHOUEN HEKISUI KILN

APRIL 2012

WILLIAM N. VALAVANIS COLLECTION
ROCHESTER, NEW YORK

No. 23 – Golden Full-Moon Maple

The most colorful and widely grown variety of Full-moon maple is the Golden full-moon maple. It has bright golden foliage in spring which turns lime green and continues throughout the remaining growing season. Red flowers are often produced in spring and remain on the tree all summer. They are generally winter hardy in the upstate New York region, but require additional protection when container grown. Diseases are often the cause of weakening Golden full-moon maples and should be sprayed with a fungicide in early spring to avoid the dreaded Verticillium wilt, which is commonly referred to as the "black death." It is best to maintain a clean area where the bonsai are kept and to dip pruning tools in alcohol between trimming Japanese maple bonsai.

Select specimens for training carefully to avoid swollen graft unions. The Golden full-moon maple is propagated by grafting. Although I have successfully rooted this cultivar to eliminate ugly graft unions, the cuttings were difficult to overwinter.

This Golden full-moon maple bonsai was completely container grown from a young grafted tree. Fred Stanzel trained the bonsai for approximately ten years and I obtained the tree in 2005.

The lower main branches of this Golden full-moon maple bonsai are opposite to each other and confusing. It would have been easy to simply prune the lower right branch, but I wanted to keep as much foliage on the tree to increase the trunk thickness. In a few years the branch can be easily eliminated. Rather than pruning one of the opposite branches I tried a technique I often use with narrow leaf evergreen species to lower branches.

I have not tried this technique on deciduous species because their wood is hard and easily splits. In March 2010 I carefully cut part way through the branch and pulled it away from the trunk downward. The exposed area was filled in with Cut Paste to retain moisture and promote healing and the branch was

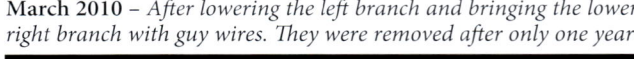

October 2008 – *The autumn coloring of the Golden full-moon maple is dependable. The lower opposite branching is confusing and must be corrected. The contrast of the orange leaves and blue container is excellent.*

secured with a guy wire. The technique was a success and I have now used it frequently on deciduous as well as narrow leaf evergreens. A video of this technique can be located on YouTube at: http://www.youtube.com/watch?v=yGOqHLpk_Ok

March 2010 – *The lower left branch was cut part way through to the trunk and lowered with a guy wire in March before leaves appeared.*

March 2010 – *After lowering the left branch and bringing the lower right branch with guy wires. They were removed after only one year.*

NO. 23 – GOLDEN FULL-MOON MAPLE
Acer japonicum 'Aureum' *or* 'Kinkakure'

HEIGHT 29 INCHES ▲ CONTAINER: JAPANESE TOKONAME-WARE FROM THE SUIHOEN HEKISUI KILN

MAY 2011

WILLIAM N. VALAVANIS COLLECTION
ROCHESTER, NEW YORK

NO. 24 – GOLDEN FULL-MOON MAPLE

This Golden full-moon maple bonsai was started from a young grafted tree and trained in the literati style. The graft union is beginning to swell on the lower trunk, and although a bit unsightly, shows the age and antiquity of the bonsai. The specimen was grown in a training pot for a few years to establish vigor, then planted in the ground for fifteen years before potting into a deep bonsai container.

Over thirty years have now been spent cultivating this tree, and although at first glance might not appear to be a fine quality bonsai, it does have the quiet and elegant beauty typical of literati style bonsai. The age and cultivation in a bonsai container can been seen when appreciating and respecting the elegance of this Golden full-moon maple bonsai.

October 2012 – *This bonsai has several pleasing viewing points. The lower trunk and surface roots are only part of the components of bonsai.*

October 2012 – *An unusual shape bonsai deserves an unusual shape container. A friend found this American container in Rochester, New York.*

NO. 24 – GOLDEN FULL-MOON MAPLE
Acer japonicum 'Aureum' *or* 'Kinkakure'

HEIGHT 30 INCHES ▲ CONTAINER: AMERICAN

OCTOBER 2012

WILLIAM N. VALAVANIS COLLECTION
ROCHESTER, NEW YORK

NO. 25 – FULL-MOON MAPLE

The Full-moon maple, like other maple varieties have sympodial branching where the tip bud is dominant and grows longer than the subordinate small branches and twigs. I have observed and studied the sympodial branching of maple, azalea, beech, enkianthus, gardenia, dwarf black olive and dogwood and often train these species in one of the cascade styles because of their natural and conducive formation to grow long horizontal branches.

In 1970-1971 I sold most of my bonsai to finance my year study in Omiya Bonsai Village in Japan. Upon returning home in 1972 I went nursery shopping on Long Island at Environmentals, a nursery specializing in dwarf conifers and other unusual species owned by James Cross. He had several plants he was experimenting with for bonsai which he select from the thousands of plants which passed through his large nursery. He gave me his collection of plants and among them was this Full-moon maple. It is a select seedling with smaller leaves than the common Full-moon and they are slightly dissected.

I have discovered that this species tends to have attractive colorful flowers in spring, which often persist and develop the typical winged seed or samaras of maples. The wings allow for seed distribution further away from the parent tree.

Originally this Full-moon maple was growing in a three gallon pot and had the long horizontal trunk. It was potted into a bonsai container and the long lower trunk was wired, as well as the shorter upper trunk. Since this variety is fast growing it is important to carefully monitor the wire to prevent scaring of the bark. At one time an iron rod was used to straighten the lower trunk for shaping.

In spring, I trim the center bud from each branch tip which is larger and fatter. Removing the vigorous leader bud slows down the growth a bit but more importantly gives more strength to the buds behind. This will encourage dense branching and twigs.

It is interesting to note that the length of the lower main trunk has not increased for nearly forty years. The trunk thickness has gotten bigger and the trunk has aged which presents an aged feeling to the impact this bonsai presents. Like my other cascade style maple bonsai, I am careful when moving this tree to prevent damage to the beautiful delicate lower trunk.

This Full-moon maple is being trained in the two line cascade style and is attractive in both spring and autumn when it consistently provides viewers with striking orange red foliage. It was displayed in the 2010 2ND U. S. National Bonsai Exhibition.

May 1999 – *The branching pattern for maples is named sympodial where the terminal bud is more vigorous and can be easily seen.*

April 1999 – *Small compact foliage and branching is being developed by removing the terminal bud in early spring.*

April 2006 – *A deeper fine quality Chinese container was used for this bonsai. The flower pattern of the container sides is good for this species.*

May 2008 – *As the leaves mature they create a full silhouette of delicate foliage accented by beautiful red flowers.*

April 2010 – *Every few years it is necessary to thin out the twigs to allow for sunlight and air to reach the inner branches.*

June 2010 – *The tree design, aged bark, trunk and surface root region harmonize together to present a quiet feeling in this classical bonsai.*

NO. 25 – FULL-MOON MAPLE
Acer japonicum

TOP TO BOTTOM 36 INCHES ▲ CONTAINER: CHINESE, CANTON-WARE

OCTOBER 2011

WILLIAM N. VALAVANIS COLLECTION
ROCHESTER, NEW YORK

NO. 26 – TRIDENT MAPLE

When grown from seed many species come true. However, some species, including maples, can vary considerably in their growth, foliage, flowers, fruit or winter hardiness. Japanese maples vary considerably, especially in their foliage. Propagators carefully study these variants and if desirable will watch to see how the new plant grows, and perhaps select it as a new cultivar.

Trident maples, on the other hand, generally come true to seed and there is little variation. Slight differences, which most horticulturists would never perceive, often make a difference to bonsai artists. In Japan I saw a Japanese grey bark elm which was prized because the leaf angle was only a bit different and had an impact to the design.

When training Trident maples for bonsai there are two types, large leaf with thick twigs, and the small leaf with fine thin twigs. Most bonsai are of the small leaf variety, but often a large leaf plant is desired, especially for bigger bonsai. Small leaves can be developed on the large leaf variety, but it takes continued leaf defoliation and bud pinching.

In 1988 I got a flat of three year old Trident maple seedlings from Miniature Plant Kingdom in Sebastopol, California. All were growing in small four inch containers and were about the same size. Among all the seedlings two looked different and I kept them for study. Even though they had large leaves, the surface roots were good.

The two selected Trident maples were potted into small bonsai containers and trained for bonsai. This tree has never been drastically pruned, it has been lovingly grown and pinched. Each spring considerable time is spent washing and arranging the surface root display. The pot shapes have varied according to my taste. Finally I selected a fine quality Japanese container of Tokonameware. This Trident maple is the finest from the original group of young seedlings and I have enjoyed training and appreciating the fine form, especially the outstanding lower trunk and surface root region. It has great promise for developing into a masterpiece bonsai.

April 2007 – *The bonsai was transplanted into a shallow container to emphasize the trunk size. The coarse twigs are evenly distributed around the tapering trunk.*

October 2011 – *This outstanding bonsai looks good from both sides. This back view also has excellent surface roots. The bonsai was not defoliated this season and developed larger foliage.*

October 2012 – *In early June the bonsai was completely defoliated and kept in a full sun exposure. Trident maple foliage is thicker than Japanese maple and can withstand more sunlight.*

NO. 26 – TRIDENT MAPLE
Acer buergerianum

HEIGHT 23 INCHES ▲ CONTAINER: JAPANESE TOKONAME-WARE FROM THE SUISHOUEN HEKISUI KILN

NOVEMBER 2012

WILLIAM N. VALAVANIS COLLECTION
ROCHESTER, NEW YORK

NO. 27 – TRIDENT MAPLE

This Trident maple was initially started by Brussel Martin, Brussel's Bonsai Nursery, Olive Branch, Mississippi. During a buying trip in 1988 Doug Taylor purchased the large size developing bonsai. We trained it together and the bonsai was responding to leaf cutting for developing additional branching and smaller foliage. In 1992 a mouse got into Mr. Taylor's over wintering poly house and ate the top of all the heavy surface roots. It was scared up pretty bad and he did not want it. So after trading, this damaged Trident maple bonsai was added to my collection. I carefully made clean cuts using a sharp chisel around the chewed up root areas and then sealed with Cut Paste. Ten years later there is no evidence of scaring, as new bark has completely covered the wounds. The surface roots are quite impressive for this large heavy bonsai.

NO. 27 – TRIDENT MAPLE
Acer bugerianum

HEIGHT 35 INCHES ▲ CONTAINER: CHINESE

OCTOBER 2001

WILLIAM N. VALAVANIS COLLECTION
ROCHESTER, NEW YORK

NO. 28 – TRIDENT MAPLE

This Trident maple was container grown in Florida and was approximately ten years old when I brought it to my garden in May 1983. During a workshop Harvey Carapella and I carefully inspected the root base, which was the best part of this tree.

The entire top was drastically pruned and the remaining stump was potted into a deep training pot with coarse soil to encourage fast growth of both the roots and new branches.

The tree grew well and has developed into a beautiful bonsai with an impressive base. It was displayed in the 2005 Upstate New York Bonsai Exhibition where it received the coveted Member's Choice Award in honor and memory of Yuji Yoshimura for his contributions to the art of classical bonsai.

May 1983 – The original tree was approximately five feet tall. The trunk was allowed to grow to produce the powerful base. It was drastically pruned then the trunk and roots were washed prior to potting.

 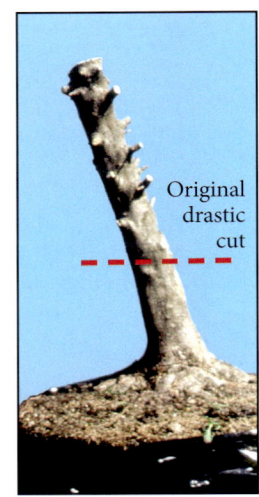

Original drastic cut

The original drastic cut for this Trident maple has healed and smoothed over. All other scars have now been covered with fresh new bark.

May 2005 – This award winning bonsai shows the fresh new growth which is tinged red and presents a beautiful display.

NO. 28 – TRIDENT MAPLE
Acer buergerianum

HEIGHT 23 INCHES ▲ CONTAINER: CHINESE XIXING-WARE

MAY 2008

HARVEY B. CARAPELLA COLLECTION
ROCHESTER, NEW YORK

NO. 29 – TRIDENT MAPLE

Several Trident maples were started in March 1983 after a buying trip to Tennessee. This bonsai was developed from that group. It did not have the heaviest trunk, but did show a promising future surface root development.

The initial techniques for pruning, potting and development are described on pages 28-31. After potting into the clay training pot the soil surface was covered with a thick layer of chopped long-fiber sphagnum moss which will prevent soil from splashing on the newly washed trunk, insulate from heat and cold and provide a bit of moisture to encourage the development of surface roots. It is easy to chop the long-fiber moss by moistening first then making a tight fist. Finally use pruning shears to cut the moss into fine pieces. The new branches were trained and later on the heavy branch on the right and trunk were reduced to improve the design of the bonsai.

In 1986 the bonsai was first planted into a bright yellow bonsai container for a few years, then into a shallow container. In 2007 the Trident maple suffered from a fungus and lost several branches which have been regrown with thinner limbs. It was potted into a large deep unglazed oval container with straight sides which was better suited for evergreen species.

This bonsai was featured on the cover of the 2002/NO. 3 issue of *International BONSAI* and was selected as one of the top 100 bonsai in the 2002 World Bonsai Contest held in Japan.

March 1983 – *After drastic pruning the trunk, branches and roots the stump was potted into a clay deep training pot. Note the deep water space and soil covering with chopped up long-fiber sphagnum moss used to maintain additional moisture and encourage surface roots.*

May 1992 – *The deep dark blue bonsai container is suitable for this bonsai with the thick trunk and full canopy of foliage. This bonsai was defoliated annually since 1986 to encourage additional fine twigs, small foliage and a brighter autumn coloring.*

October 2001 – *Good weather and cultural growing created a bright autumn color. Note the small foliage evenly throughout the bonsai.*

November 2001 – *After leaf drop the true structure and design can be appreciated. Note the original drastic cut is beginning to disappear.*

March 2002 – *In spring before the leaves appear the terminal bud is often removed to encourage smaller buds to develop.*

October 2008 – *In 2007 the tree suffered from a fungus disease so it was planted into a larger container and not defoliated.*

October 2012 – *Because of the rapidly expanding lower trunk and surface root region the bonsai was transplanted into a larger container to balance the massive crown. The tree lost several branches in 2007, but survived and the twigs are being regrown. Next small foliage will be developed again.*

NO. 29 – TRIDENT MAPLE
Acer buergerianum

HEIGHT 23 INCHES ▲ CONTAINER: CHINESE XIXING-WARE

MAY 2012

WILLIAM N. VALAVANIS COLLECTION
ROCHESTER, NEW YORK

NO. 30 – TRIDENT MAPLE

Usually field grown Trident maples, and many other deciduous species, have straight trunks. I got lucky finding this specimen which had movement in the lower trunk, but lacked a good surface root development. After it was established, exhibited vigorous growth and had a good fibrous root system, I grafted several young Trident maple seedlings in the front to improve the root base. Although they are straight, the end result thirty years later is better than when I started. Today, I would have used young seedlings with curved lower trunks for grafting.

This Trident maple bonsai was allowed to grow then was cut back repeatedly for a few decades to increase the number of branches, not to develop small leaves. It is not a good idea to develop small foliage in the developmental stage of a bonsai because the vigor will not be there to grow branches and small twigs. Developing small foliage causes the plant to slow down in growth and the trunk and branch thickness will not form.

The hollow area in the lower right trunk area was a problem and not part of my intended design. Every year in spring the perimeter was carefully cut with a sharp knife to stimulate the new callus tissue to form. Epoxy putty used by plumbers, which looks similar to the Japanese Cut Paste but becomes hard, was put into the hollow and shaped in a convex form to allow new bark to easily form and seal the wound. As can be seen in the last photo, the hollow is nearly covered with bark.

I was unable to grow lower back branches on this old trunk so inarch grafting was necessary. Several new shoots were allowed to grow about fifteen to twenty inches in length from upper branches the year before inarch grafting. The following spring these long flexible branches were positioned into the ideal locations for back branches. Then a chisel was used to carve a hollow depression for the new branch. It too was slightly scraped, but this is not always necessary. Then I simply used a staple gun to secure the new branches on to the old trunk. After a year or two the section of the unneeded shoot was pruned.

This Trident maple was the logo tree for the 2008 Deciduous Bonsai Symposium.

April 1983 – *The stump was first potted into a bonsai container for future development. The four prominent roots in front were grafted to improve the root spread. The hollow hole on the right was a problem and needed attention to heal because it was not suitable for my presentation of this tree as a fine quality deciduous bonsai.*

March 1998 – *The previous unglazed container was not suitable for this bonsai so an excellent glazed container was located. Note the increase of small branches and the healing hollow on the lower trunk.*

May 1998 – *When in leaf this bonsai presents a fuller and more massive effect which is in better proportion to the bonsai. New shoots were allowed to grow, then trim back for development.*

May 2003 – *The new container balances the heavy crown of the bonsai.*

July 2006 – *Small foliage is now being developed by bud pinching.*

January 2007 – *Fine twigs developing and trunk hollow beginning to cover.*

April 2007 – *A shallow container was used to emphasize the trunk size.*

May 2007 – *The new leaves grew larger in spring because of not pinching.*

July 2008 – *Small foliage developed with bud pinching in spring.*

October 2012

Small foliage has now developed on this Trident maple bonsai and is evenly distributed throughout the crown. It is necessary to continue to bud pinch to maintain the small size. Note the hollow in the lower right trunk is nearly covered by new bark, yet I still scrape the perimeter of the wound each year to stimulate the rapid formation of bark. The hard Epoxy Putty in the hollow gives the callus something to grow over rather than just form callus tissue turning inward. The autumn color this season was good for this bonsai and the multi colors were evenly distributed in the crown and contrast nicely with the green moss and white container.

Improving Surface Root Display For Deciduous Species

This lower trunk and surface root region needs small roots between the heavy roots which were grafted onto the trunk over thirty years ago. Note the new callus tissue forming on the hollow area on the right. The Cut Paste is shrinking.

Use a sharp chisel to make a smooth cut in the area where new roots are desired. A knife can also work but might be difficult to get into small areas especially under the trunk.

Moisten the newly exposed area with water to help the absorption of a root inducing powder. I use Hormodin 3, but others can also work. Then dust the area with the root inducing powder. Do not apply too much, only a dusting will work. Too much might inhibit new root formation. Finally pack tightly with moist long-fiber sphagnum moss which will create an environment for new root formation. Often I will put a hairpin of wire to hold the long-fiber sphagnum moss from moving. Additional Cut Paste has been added to the hollow area at the conclusion of this technique to promote rapid covering with new bark.

NO. 30 – TRIDENT MAPLE
Acer buergerianum

HEIGHT 22 INCHES ▲ CONTAINER: CHINESE XIXING-WARE

OCTOBER 2012

WILLIAM N. VALAVANIS COLLECTION
ROCHESTER, NEW YORK

NO. 31 – TRIDENT MAPLE

In February 1993 during a lecture tour through Georgia, North Carolina and Virginia, I presented a program at a bonsai conference in Atlanta, Georgia. After my program I sold my demonstration tree and purchased this Trident maple. It was field grown in Florida and less than ten years old. This species grows quite fast, especially in warm climates. Someone was showing a battery powered small chain saw so I borrowed it and drastically pruned the Trident maple, leaving only a stump. I still had some money left so purchased a large Chinese container which would fit the tree. The tree was freshly potted so I went into the parking lot and bare rooted the stump, leaving the soil in the hotel landscape. The roots needed to be kept moist until I returned home the following week so I got a large plastic garbage bag from the hotel, shredded moistened newspaper, wrapped up the stump and put it in my car.

My next stop was a program with Yuji Yoshimura in Charlotte, North Carolina. When he saw the stump he asked "What are you going to do with that stump?" I replied "Make a bonsai" Then he said "Good Luck!" I'm assuming Yuji Yoshimura's luck was good for me, because twenty years later the basic structure has been developed for a future bonsai. Detailed illustrated instructions on how I initially developed this bonsai, as well as other deciduous species can be located on page 28.

November 2008 – *This major scar, over four inches wide, has completely healed in approximately ten years. Quicker covering of new bark will happen if the top and bottom of the wound are pointed and tapered toward the center, not rounded. For deciduous species make a deep concave cut and seal to maintain moisture so the cambium layer does not dry out.*

February 1993 – *This newly potted Trident maple grown in the field in Florida for only ten years. It was approximately four feet tall and three feet wide, before drastic pruning.*

February 1993 – *A small battery operated chain saw was used to remove all the branches so I could get it into my car. The stump is still approximately four feet tall, but only five inches wide.*

May 1993 – After trimming and wiring the new shoots down. Very few, if any, shoots were removed. Final branch selection can be done later, now the main goal is to get the plant vigorous and shape branches.

May 1993 – In only two months the stump suddenly became a bush. Now is the time to wire all the new shoots down because it will be difficult to lower when they become heavy.

June 1995 – After thinning and reducing the foliage. The top section of the tree has been trimmed more than the left and right side where growth is needed. A branch on the right has been selected to be the thickest so it is allowed to grow wild, then will be cut back.

June 1995 – The new growth before trimming and thinning two years later.

February 1995 – *All the branches are the same age. Branch thickness should differ to provide interest and variety to the bonsai design. In order to get different sizes some branches must be allowed to grow wild to thicken. The first branch on the right has been selected to be the heaviest so it is not pruned.*

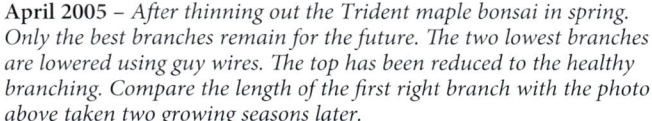

October 2006 – *The newly developed heavy branch on the right was allowed to grow. Even in the cold climate of Rochester, New York, it is not unusual to grow branches four to six feet in only one growing season when grown in a container. The remaining branches of the bonsai are continually trimmed to maintain the silhouette and prevent thick branches from forming in the upper crown.*

April 2005 – *Every spring the branches are thinned out to eliminate those which are crossing, overly thick and growing straight. Although the bonsai has many twigs, they are not delicate and must be thinned out and shortened for future development. A slightly larger container of a different color and design was selected for the bonsai.*

April 2005 – *After thinning out the Trident maple bonsai in spring. Only the best branches remain for the future. The two lowest branches are lowered using guy wires. The top has been reduced to the healthy branching. Compare the length of the first right branch with the photo above taken two growing seasons later.*

Left–
March 1993 – *My two sons, Nicholas (4 years) left and Christopher (2 1/2 years) helped wash the roots when initially pruning and potting the Trident maple.*

Right–
October 2012 – *My two sons, Nicholas (23 years) left and Christopher (21 years) helped move the now heavy Trident maple bonsai.*

NO. 31 – TRIDENT MAPLE
Acer buergerianum

HEIGHT 3 INCHES ▲ CONTAINER: CHINESE XIXING-WARE

OCTOBER 2012

WILLIAM N. VALAVANIS COLLECTION
ROCHESTER, NEW YORK

No. 32 – Trident Maple

This is one of the several Trident maples which were started in March 1983 upon returning home from a buying trip to Tennessee. The tree featured here was one of the smaller specimens which was developing well and the basic branching was established. The twigs were just beginning to form.

My assistant Brenta Sullivan liked the tree and added it to her collection which was rapidly growing in the early 1990s. She assisted me daily and used the techniques learned in my studio for her bonsai at home. All of her bonsai were regularly brought to my workshops for check ups.

The initial techniques for pruning, potting and development are described on pages 28-31. She continued to develop the bonsai and displayed it several times in the Upstate New York Bonsai Exhibition held in Rochester, New York.

Mrs. Sullivan gave me her Trident maple bonsai in 2004 when she was no longer able to care for it. This bonsai has been used for several transplanting and trimming demonstrations.

May 1998 – This Trident maple bonsai was displayed in several Upstate New York Bonsai Exhibitions. The first branch on the right was a bit weak and needed additional foliage to create balance. It was allowed to lengthen a bit before trimming back to the silhouette.

April 2009 – *In spring new buds swell and foliage begins to slowly open. In order to maintain a compact shape I often trim back the opening buds and shorten the branches a bit. Here the buds are ready for this technique. After trimming the bonsai is ready for transplanting or placing in a full sun location in the garden.*

April 2009 – *After trimming back the opening buds and reducing the length of the branches the bonsai is ready for transplanting. This timing is excellent for cold climates like western New York where late spring frosts are common which can quickly damage and sometimes kill the bonsai. If transplanted too soon the bonsai might be damaged by frost.*

July 2009 – *During the summer vigorous new shoots lengthen and need trimming to increase the number of branches. It is important not to continually trim back to one location because that area might get heavy.*

July 2009 – *After new growth trimming the Trident maple bonsai looks neater. Large leaves are also removed at this time and throughout the growing season as well. The removal of large leaves will allow additional sunlight and air to reach the inner branches.*

October 2008 – *Autumn brings different colors to this Trident maple which varies from year to year. This year the autumn coloring was not as spectacular as other years.*

October 2012 – *In late summer deciduous bonsai are rotated 180 degrees every few days for good even autumn coloring. Sometimes the bonsai are moved in the garden so they can obtain brighter light.*

NO. 32 – TRIDENT MAPLE
Acer buergerianum

HEIGHT 22 INCHES ▲ CONTAINER: JAPANESE SHIGARAKI-WARE

NOVEMBER 2012

WILLIAM N. VALAVANIS COLLECTION
ROCHESTER, NEW YORK

NO. 33 – TRIDENT MAPLE

Originally this Trident maple was eight to ten feet tall growing in a Tennessee nursery field in the mid-1970s. It was drastically pruned and potted into a plastic bonsai pot by Brussel Martin. I purchased the tree in 1979 for $125 because the trunk interested me. The heavy original branches were not pruned and looked out of balance during the winter. In March 1980 I started all over again and bare rooted the tree, drastically pruned the top and roots. Additional information on the initial training techniques can be located beginning on page 28.

Looking back now over thirty years later, it was probably wasteful to drastically prune such a tree and begin all over again. I wanted to create a fine quality bonsai, not live with thick poor branching. Often it is preferable not to waste time, but to continue with the original artist's form.

The new shoots were vigorous and quickly lengthened. It is important to get their positions lowered for future branch formation. If allowed to grow upright and wired down at a later time the base of the branch might break or will have an undesirable convex formation.

Each year the bonsai was allowed to grow without pruning and often reached four feet in height. It was only pruned yearly in spring. Since all the branches are the same age one branch was allowed to grow untrimmed for thickening.

The bonsai was first potted into a deep bonsai container in March 1985 and new shoots were trimmed to form the basic structure. In June 1988 this Trident maple bonsai was potted into a blue glazed oval container, which was shallow, but the soil dried out quickly because of the massive crown and needed to be transplanted yearly. In February 1995 the bonsai was transplanted into a white glazed rectangular container because of the straight trunk and looked better because the straight trunk complimented the straight lines of the container, but more importantly, did not dry out as often.

As the bonsai matured, the heavy roots on the left became prominent and I decided to refine the design by tilting the trunk to the right to present an informal upright design. Originally the crown of the bonsai was trained in a narrow rounded silhouette. It was reshaped into a rounded shape to present the feeling of a mature natural tree.

May 1980 – *After drastic pruning and initial potting. All pruning wounds were sealed with Tree Coat, an asphalt base tree wound sealant because Japanese Cut Paste was not invented at that time. Small new shoots can be seen emerging from the stump which was washed before potting in a coarse size soil mix.*

Since the design was changed a new container was necessary to better balance the tree and pot. A light blue glazed oval container with thicker sides was selected to provide the necessary balance of the now informal upright bonsai.

This Trident maple was featured on the cover of the 2002/ NO. 2 issue of *International BONSAI* with additional information and photos.

July 1980 – *The shoots before trimming and wiring.* **July 1980** – *After trimming and wiring.* **September 1980** – *Growth after one growing season.*

July 1980 – *Multiple new shoots before wiring horizontal.*

July 1980 – *After wiring new shoots and pruning one in the center.*

March 1983 – *New shoots were allowed to grow then trimmed in spring.*

April 1985 – *After trimming and potting into the first bonsai container.*

October 2001 – *Full silhouette of colorful foliage is too heavy for the pot.*

November 2001 – *The leafless beauty of the bonsai is in balance with the pot.*

May 2006 – *An oval container with thicker sides compliments the newly trained wider rounded silhouette of the crown.*

April 2007 – *Fine twigs developing in the crown which has been shaped into a wider rounded shape.*

October 2012 – *The full crown of colorful foliage compliments the light blue glazed container. The balance of the foliage, trunk and container are excellent.*

NO. 33 – TRIDENT MAPLE
Acer buergerianum

HEIGHT 21 INCHES ▲ CONTAINER: CHINESE

NOVEMBER 2012

WILLIAM N. VALAVANIS COLLECTION
ROCHESTER, NEW YORK

NO. 34 – SEIJU ELM

There are many different cultivars of Chinese elm trained for bonsai. The cultivar Hokkaido has extremely tiny foliage, actually too small because they do not look real. It is considered a bit difficult to grow and overwinter, especially in cold climates.

In September 1975 a specimen of Hokkaido Chinese elm mutated and was selected by H. Carl and Shin Young, Seiju-en Bonsai Garden in Lodi, California. This unusual branch had foliage larger than Hokkaido, thick corky bark and grew much easier, and is winter hardy in cold climates. They named it Seiju Chinese elm after their garden. Thousands of cuttings and air layers were taken and were grown in the fields where once grape vines grew.

In 1977 Mr. Young took 3,000 cuttings and planted them in his field. In 1981 I selected this specimen because of the unusual nearly straight trunk which is not common. The tree was potted directly into a bonsai container and trained. The trunk thickened considerably and I allowed the two lowest branches to remain to help the thickening.

The dedicated trimming of the new shoots whenever they lengthened contributed into the outstanding ramification of the developed bonsai. This Seiju elm bonsai was often displayed and comments were made about removing one of the two lowest branches. They did not bother me and I liked them, so they remained on the bonsai.

In 1992 Corin Tomlinson was my apprentice from England and we discussed the branches. I finally decided to remove both of the lowest branches. He liked the branches and rooted one of them to take to his father's bonsai nursery in England. The bonsai first declined in vigor for a few seasons then recovered and grew.

This Seiju elm was the logo tree for the 1994 Elm Bonsai Symposium and was featured on the cover of the 1999/NO. 4 issue of *International BONSAI*.

July 1983 – *The field grown tree was potted and trained in a bonsai container. When the bonsai became too large for the container another pot of the same style and color was ordered directly from Japan.*

March 1984 – *Many small twigs were formed by the continued trimming of the new shoots.*

June 1985 – *The small foliage, continually trimmed remained small and was attractive in summer.*

NO. 34 – SEIJU ELM
Ulmus parvifolia 'Seiju'

HEIGHT 30 INCHES ▲ CONTAINER: JAPANESE TOKONAME-WARE FROM THE REIHO KILN

APRIL 1992

WILLIAM N. VALAVANIS COLLECTION
ROCHESTER, NEW YORK

NO. 35– DWARF CHINESE ELM

This is one of the many dwarf cultivars of Chinese elm. It has small dark green, narrow leaves which are serrated. The bark becomes quite thick, corky and adds dimension and interest to the bonsai design. As it ages, the bark often has reddish highlights. This cultivar grows larger than Seiju Chinese elm, but the foliage is narrow and interesting too.

This Dwarf Chinese elm began as a cutting I rooted in 1973. A few years earlier Tony Mihalic, Wildwood Gardens, Chardon, Ohio, gave me a small cutting of this dwarf cultivar and I made numerous cuttings from the original for propagation and selling through my second catalog listing dwarf and unusual cultivars for bonsai.

After rooting the young plant was grown in a three inch, one quart, one gallon and finally in a two gallon can. It has been completely container grown. As it grew I took numerous cuttings and distributed them throughout the country.

In 1987 I planted a cutting from the original stock plant in the ground for taking cuttings. It is now over eighteen feet in height and has a trunk diameter of over twelve inches, covered with thick corky bark. One of the branches has reverted to the common Cork-bark Chinese elm and has been eliminated to maintain the dwarf cultivar. Cuttings are now taken from this plant for future bonsai.

The trunk of the Dwarf Chinese elm bonsai continued to grow and thicken. The original bend in the trunk has now disappeared. In 1985 it was planted into a shallow white glazed bonsai container. The trunk continued to become massive and was later transplanted into the larger unglazed brown oval container which was deeper and better balanced the silhouette.

As the trunk continued to thicken, so did the branches. Although the first two branches are not opposite, they are close together. Now they appear to be opposite which is not considered to be good classical bonsai design. Rather than prune one of them, I decided to pull the first branch down using guy wires. This solution has solved the problem for the near future.

August 1987

The first potting for this bonsai was a shallow unglazed rectangular container. This Dwarf Chinese elm bonsai was displayed in the 1987 Midwest Bonsai Exhibit held in Chicago, Illinois.

April 1999 – *The delicate fine twigging of this bonsai can be enjoyed in early spring as the buds open.*

May 1999 – *Small leaves are lighter green than when they mature to a rich dark green later in late spring.*

April 2006

Three copper guy wires were used to carefully pull down the first branch on the right. Also a few pieces of bark were removed from the bottom of the first left branch so the two lower branches do not appear to be opposite. Note how thick the bottom of the trunk has grown and now looks massive with the thick corky bark.

NO. 35 – DWARF CHINESE ELM
Ulmus parvifolia 'Yatsubusa'

HEIGHT 24 INCHES ▲ CONTAINER: JAPANESE, TOKONAME-WARE

MAY 2006

WILLIAM N. VALAVANIS COLLECTION
ROCHESTER, NEW YORK

NO. 36 – CHINESE ELM

In 1988 several hundred Chinese elm seedlings were obtained from a nursery in Alabama. Although all the seedlings were the same age, they varied in height from six inches to over four feet. Each seedling was individually potted for future training as single trunk or group planting style bonsai.

In March 1990 I selected several specimens, mostly in one gallon pots, and created an idealized view of a distant elm forest. I wanted to see how much root pruning young Chinese elm seedlings could withstand. Despite the fact that each seedling was drastically root pruned, all survived and thrived. This was a valuable lesson for me which I have shared with students. Nearly all the roots of young deciduous seedlings are routinely drastically pruned, sometimes leaving no fibrous roots, only a tap root stub.

I initially wanted to place the base of the trunks closer together but did not. Originally I had planned on repotting the Chinese elm forest to position the trunks closer together, but never had the time. However, when comparing the original photograph with the most current it appears at though the thickening trunks took care of the spacing problem.

A larger and deeper white glazed Korean bonsai container was selected in 1999 for this bonsai because of the rapidly growing silhouette of fine branches. In 2002 a fine quality Japanese container was hand selected in Tokoname, Japan, at the Yamaaki Kiln for this bonsai. I like containers with an outer lip for deciduous species. This pot also had thicker side walls to provide visual strength for the increased foliage mass.

It is important to remember that each seedling is genetically different. Even though all the Chinese elm seedlings originated from the same source they vary. In autumn this is most apparent because the trees change to different colors. Note that two specimens, front left and rear right, have reddish autumn coloring while the other specimens are characteristically yellow, the color of most elms. Although this variegation in a forest is beautiful, I think it looks messy and prefer a more quiet appearance with all seedlings of identical color, but this is personal taste, based on my background and bonsai philosophy.

This Chinese elm forest has slowed down in vigor. In the early years after assembling the forest a yearly transplanting was necessary. Now twenty five years later this bonsai is only transplanted every four or five years because the water still freely drains and the trees are healthy.

Originally I created a "distant view" forest perspective using small thin seedlings emphasizing the entire silhouette of the planting, rather than a "near view" perspective where heavy trunk are prominent and individual trees are featured. It looks like my original design has changed due to the thicknesses of the trunks.

This Chinese elm was used for the 1998 Landscape Bonsai Symposium and was displayed in the 2008 1ST U. S. National Bonsai Exhibition.

It is important to remember that bonsai is a living and changing horticultural art form. If you do not like your original bonsai creation, do not give up, but rather, quietly wait, everything changes and often the outcome is worth the patience.

March 1990 – *Immediately after planting in a shallow container. Basically only the tree heights and diameters were considered, not the branching which is easily developed.*

May 1990 – *Fresh new leaves quickly appeared and the trees grew well.*

April 1993 – *Branches are beginning to develop.*

June 1999 – *A Korean container with incurving sides was used.*

November 2002 – *A deeper container was needed because of the silhouette.*

January 2003 – *Fine twigs are developing throughout the planting.*

May 2003 – *The thickening trunks appear to be closer together.*

October 2008 – *Displayed in the 2008 2ⁿᴰ U. S. National Bonsai Exhibition.*

November 2008 – *Note the two trees with reddish foliage.*

NO. 36 – CHINESE ELM
Ulmus parvifolia

HEIGHT 30 INCHES ▲ CONTAINER: JAPANESE TOKONAME-WARE FROM THE YAMAAKI KILN

JANUARY 2009

WILLIAM N. VALAVANIS COLLECTION
ROCHESTER, NEW YORK

no. 37 – Red Leaf Hornbeam

The young new shoots which have red stems is the reason this species is commonly named Red leaf hornbeam. It also has the common name Loose flowering hornbeam because of the interesting fruit which form in late spring, persist throughout the summer and mature in autumn.

Before the fruit form the entire tree is full of long flowers in early spring. This bonsai, like many deciduous species does not abundantly flower and fruit yearly. It rests a year before producing a multitude of flowers. Knowing this fact can be helpful when preparing bonsai for display. Flower buds can be easily removed and the tree will rest and build up energy to produce bountiful flowers and fruit during the following season.

This Red leaf hornbeam began as a young seedling which I have container grown for over thirty five years. The heavy and powerful surface roots with striped bark have been slowly growing. It has grown well and has developed the characteristic striped muscular bark pattern hornbeams are know for which require decades. As this bonsai was developing the first branch on the right died and the callus formed around the wound. When in leaf this feature is not visible and during the dormant season adds interest. As can be seen in the winter season photos this bonsai has never been drastically pruned. It has been slowly trained into a fine classic bonsai.

In order to improve this bonsai according to my design, emphasize the trunk size and create a more rounded crown the top was pruned in spring 2007. It was also transplanted into a larger and deeper container with straight lines to compliment the trunk.

The fresh new foliage, combined with the long interesting fruit have made this bonsai popular in exhibitions. In May 2006 it received the Member's Choice Award at the Upstate New York Bonsai Exhibition presented in memory and honor of Yuji Yoshimura for his endeavors to promote the understanding of bonsai. In August 2006 this bonsai won the First Prize Award in the Professional Division in the Midwest Bonsai Exhibit held in Chicago, Illinois.

In June 2011 this Red leaf hornbeam also received the Best Of Show Award at the combined convention of Bonsai Clubs International and the American Bonsai Society held in Louisville, Kentucky. This Red leaf hornbeam was displayed in the 2008 1ST U. S. National Bonsai Exhibition as well as the 2010 2ND U. S. National Bonsai Exhibition where it was the logo.

May 1997 –
Planted in this Chinese bonsai container, the bonsai slowly began to develop into a masterpiece.

February 2006 – *Flower buds before opening.*

March 2006 – *Full blossoms open in early spring.*

May 2006 – *Long fruit develop in late spring.*

April 2007 – The bonsai was transplanted into a larger container which compliments the shape of the trunk and balances the silhouette. The basic structure can be enjoyed during the winter dormant season.

October 2008 – As displayed in the 2008 2ND U. S. National Bonsai Exhibition. Here the bonsai is beginning to change color and has a few mature fruit with viable seed.

April 2010 – Young new leaves opening with fruit beginning to develop. Shoots with fruit must not be bud pinched if fruit are to be enjoyed. Each year the flowering and fruiting timing varies according to the weather.

April 2011 – The Red leaf hornbeam in full flower. The long beautiful flowers are not fragrant and are pollen laden which quickly go flying when the wind blows or if the bonsai is moved.

NO. 37 – RED LEAF HORNBEAM
Carpinus laxiflora

HEIGHT 33 INCHES ▲ CONTAINER: JAPANESE TOKONAME-WARE FROM THE REIHO KILN

MAY 2009

WILLIAM N. VALAVANIS COLLECTION
ROCHESTER, NEW YORK

No. 38 – Korean Hornbeam

Several different Korean hornbeam species are trained for bonsai because of their small foliage and thick muscular trunks. The finest and oldest Korean hornbeam masterpieces in Japan originally were collected in Korea, imported to Japan and trained to the Japanese standards.

I have made several trips to Korea to see bonsai and how they are trained. In the late 1990s I made yearly trips to purchase collected as well as nursery grown bonsai. Many were sold bare root upon their arrival in my garden.

This Korean hornbeam was collected in the mountains of Korea, probably in the early 1990s. I imported two large crates of collected Korean stumps in the late 1990s and this specimen interested me because of the tapering trunk. It had a few thin branches at that time.

The tree was first established in a large deep bonsai pot to provide enough moisture and soil to encourage vigorous vegetative growth. Continued trimming of the new shoots created fine twig ramification which is enjoyed during the winter.

Several different colored containers have been used for this Korean hornbeam bonsai. Currently it is in a yellow glazed Chinese container. Although I think the color is interesting I'm not pleased with the size nor the shape. Many factors must be considered when selecting containers and my views are explained further in this book.

May 2005 – *After establishing the bonsai in a training pot the Korean hornbeam was planted in a dark blue glazed Japanese container.*

January 2007 – *Continually trimming the new shoots develops many fine twigs. The large pruning scars are beginning to cover.*

November 2010 – *The crown is becoming massive so a larger and deeper container was selected to balance the composition.*

December 2010 – *Many fine twigs have developed during the past ten years and can be enjoyed in winter.*

August 2011– *The color of the new yellow container is pleasing during the summer because of the contrasting foliage color.*

October 2012 – *Although the autumn coloring is bright it is not emphasized because of the same color container.*

NO. 38 – KOREAN HORNBEAM
Acer turczaninowii

HEIGHT 21 INCHES ▲ CONTAINER: CHINESE XIXING-WARE

NOVEMBER 2012

WILLIAM N. VALAVANIS COLLECTION
ROCHESTER, NEW YORK

NO. 39 – JAPANESE HORNBEAM

Japanese hornbeams are different than the Red leaf and Korean varieties because of their foliage, fruit and vigor. This species has larger foliage which has attractive distinctive veins which in autumn always becomes bright golden yellow. The fruit are much larger and showier than the other two hornbeam species trained for bonsai. Of these three species, I have noticed that it is the fastest growing.

This bonsai began from a seed brought to the United States by H. Carl Young, Seiju-en Bonsai Garden in Lodi, California in 1963. He grew it in a container and sent it to me in 1980. I planted it in the ground for several years and later potted the tree and continued to train it for bonsai. It is interesting that the trunk did not thicken as much as expected, but rather did develop mature looking bark.

July 2011
Summertime brings large interesting pendulous fruit which add interest and a focal point to the bonsai. In autumn the fruit mature to a brown color and continue to provide something interesting to view.

NO. 39 – JAPANESE HORNBEAM
Carpinus japonica

HEIGHT 33 INCHES ▲ CONTAINER: JAPANESE TOKONAME-WARE FROM THE KOYO KILN

NOVEMBER 2011

WILLIAM N. VALAVANIS COLLECTION
ROCHESTER, NEW YORK

No. 40 – American Larch

The American larch is an excellent deciduous species which is extremely winter hardy. Larch can be successfully collected from nearby Canada as well as in the New England states to the west coast. The Japanese larch and European larch are also a popular species, as are a few others, which are native to the western area of the United States. When specimens are collected from the mountains or bogs they generally have unique shapes and make outstanding bonsai.

Larch, a deciduous conifer, has rather rugged bark which looks aged and requires a long period of time to develop. The primarily reason larch are trained for bonsai is because of the fresh, light green new growth which displays very short and neat appearing needles in early spring. Once the new growth has matured the foliage tends to be a bit too long and uneven, but still attractive. In autumn the green needles turn bright golden yellow and often persist for a long period of time after the tree goes into dormancy. Small cones are often seen on older specimens and are interesting and colorful while developing during the summer (reddish) and in winter when they mature to a light brown color.

The trunks of young larch can quickly thicken up if planted into the garden or large training pot. They are easily wired in late winter or early spring before the buds open, however, with care they can be successfully wired at other times of the year. It is important to transplant and root prune larch before or just as the new buds begin to open. Although many deciduous species can be successfully transplanted when the buds are opening or even with small foliage, the larch, unfortunately cannot. Be certain to transplant larch earlier than later for best results. Of course, repotting to change containers or trunk position can be done if the central soil mass is not disturbed.

This American larch was collected by John and Nadine Biel of Toronto, Canada, in a remote region on the Bruce peninsula in Ontario. In 1994 they gave this collected specimen to Brenta Sullivan. She worked with me to train her new American larch.

Upon inspecting the roots we rearranged several of the trunks to create a pleasing sinuous style bonsai. Since all the roots are connected and from one tree they are identical. It was first potted into a large brown unglazed bonsai container.

Mrs. Sullivan was a dedicated bonsai artist and took exquisite care of her bonsai. The American larch thrived under her tender loving care and needed to be transplanted into a different container. It was then transplanted into an blue glazed oval bonsai container because she enjoyed the autumn color contrast of the yellow needles and blue container.

Each spring it is necessary to remove some of the extra buds to avoid overcrowding. Do not remove the flowering buds because they will develop into small interesting cones.

When Mrs. Sullivan could no longer care for her bonsai she gave me the larch and I have attempted to keep it in the same general shape she created. Recently the trunks began to thicken and a larger container was necessary to provide visual balance and moisture for the root system. A deeper unglazed grey container was selected to provide a more quiet feeling, especially in autumn.

This American larch bonsai was displayed in the 2008 1ST U. S. National Bonsai Exhibition. Since the needles were a bit burned from a hot summer each one was individually removed to display the beauty of larch bonsai during the dormant season.

June 2000
The long mature needles during the growing season hide the small twigs during the summer.

May 2003
Spring is the best time to enjoy the newly opening buds of larch bonsai. The surface roots are attractive.

May 2007 – *The variety of trunk heights and thickness is excellent.*

July 2008 – *A full appearance is enjoyed during the summer.*

April 2008 – *The root system is pushing the root mass up.*
May 2011 – *A new deeper container was selected to balance the composition.*

October 2008 – *Winter beauty displayed in October.*
April 2012 – *Small emerging needles present a fresh feeling.*

NO. 40 – AMERICAN LARCH
Larix laricina

HEIGHT 28 INCHES ▲ CONTAINER: JAPANESE TOKONAME-WARE

NOVEMBER 2012

WILLIAM N. VALAVANIS COLLECTION
ROCHESTER, NEW YORK

NO. 41 – AMERICAN LARCH

There are two American larch in my bonsai collection, both collected by John and Nadine Biel from Toronto, Canada. This tree was brought to one of my workshops in 1983 and later it was given to me as a gift.

The previous American larch is trained in the sinuous style where all the trunks originate from a curved horizontal trunk, usually buried in the soil. The movement of the buried trunk adds perspective to the composition because the upright trunks can be positioned further back. The raft style is similar but the horizontal trunk is in a straight line. Most of the raft style bonsai in the country are actually sinuous style, but that name is not well known. This American larch is being trained in the raft style.

The 1999/NO. 2 issue of *International BONSAI* is on sinuous and raft style bonsai and this American larch is on the cover.

May 1993 – *The original trunk in a straight line, lying on the soil surface, can easily be appreciated.*

March 1999 – *The branches are beginning to thicken and small twigs are developing.*

May 2003 – *A small stone was inserted into the horizontal trunk to angle the horizontal trunk downward towards the right.*

May 2007 – *The delicate feeling of this bonsai has now been lost due to the noticeable thick trunks forming.*

May 2010 – *A larger and more shallow container was selected so the trunks would not seem as thick. Two branches were lowered with guy wires.*

May 2011 – *Two seasons were necessary to lower the two branches with guy wires and were removed the following spring.*

NO. 41 – AMERICAN LARCH
Larix laricina

HEIGHT 26 INCHES ▲ CONTAINER: CHINESE CANTON-WARE

MAY 2012

WILLIAM N. VALAVANIS COLLECTION
ROCHESTER, NEW YORK

NO. 42 – DAWN REDWOOD

Dawn redwood is a deciduous conifer native to China. It was rediscovered in 1940s and introduced to the western horticultural world. This fast growing tree is winter hardy and grows straight up so it is most suited for the formal upright bonsai style. They are easy to propagate from seed which is freely produced by large garden trees.

In the early 1990s I wanted to make a Dawn redwood forest. It took a few years to locate specimens with different trunk calibers. After the original forest was established in a bonsai pot I redesigned it in 2009 to create a more powerful composition. The new container has straight sides which I prefer for conifers. The forest is breathtaking in early spring as the foliage emerges and in autumn with bronze leaves.

August 2006 – *Original forest composition.*

April 2010 – *Forest newly designed in 2009.*

NO. 42 – DAWN REDWOOD
Metasequoia glyptostroboides

HEIGHT 30 INCHES ▲ CONTAINER: JAPANESE TOKONAME-WARE

JUNE 2009

WILLIAM N. VALAVANIS COLLECTION
ROCHESTER, NEW YORK

NO. 43 – EUROPEAN BEECH

The European beech is an excellent species for forest style bonsai. Although the natural leaf size is a bit larger than the popular Japanese beech, I have observed that the European beech foliage size reduces quickly. The green leaves during the summer turn bright yellow in autumn and often persist throughout the winter. This trait is natural because the old brown foliage protects the long sculptured leaf buds.

In April 1993 I got several hundred European beech seedlings from an Oregon nursery which were two, three and four years old. A variety was obtained in order to get seedlings of different trunk diameters and heights.

Although it is recommended that pre trained trees be used for forest bonsai, it is possible to create a pleasing group immediately if the material is carefully selected. Since these seedlings did not have a fibrous root system and very few, if any, branching it was easy to position them close together. Extra seedlings were planted to fill out the design and were to be removed as the plant matures and develops. During the past twenty years I have not removed any of the extra trees, but a few have died. None of the trees were wired, however, they were securely wired into the container.

This bonsai grew well and quickly became established. Over the next few years branches increased and the trunks thickened. The container became too small to aesthetically balance the tall tree heights so a larger container was selected. By using a longer container I changed the proportion of the composition by allowing additional negative space on the left side.

This bonsai continued to develop and was featured on the cover of the Winter 2000 issue of the *ABS Bonsai Journal*. In May 2001 I transplanted the European beech forest into the present white glazed Chinese container with thicker side walls and an outer lip. The thicker container balances the more massive canopy. This bonsai was displayed in the 2012 3RD U. S. National Bonsai Exhibition.

August 1993

European beech seedlings were used to create this forest. It is difficult to cluster trees tightly together when creating a forest if they have an abundance of roots. Young seedlings were used because they had few roots which allowed closer positioning to provide interest to the composition.

March 1999 – *A larger oval container was necessary for the growing beech forest. The bark is naturally becoming white.*

May 2002 – *Another container, of the same size, but with thicker walls and outward lip, was selected for the European beech forest.*

Bud Pinching Beech To Limit Growth & Reduce Foliage Size

Trim the terminal buds in early spring before they open. Carefully watch the swelling of the buds.

When the buds begin to open, but before they fully expand, grasp the center and pull the new leaves. Only leave one or two leaves.

Do not injure the remaining buds and be careful not to break other expanding buds with fingers when pulling the center.

Leaf structure after bud pinching. This technique will need to be repeated since all the buds do not open at the same time.

July 2003 – *The crown is becoming rounded and massive. Notice the general feeling of the bonsai has not changed.*

June 2012 – *The fine branches have developed considerably smaller foliage than the common European beech.*

NO. 43 – EUROPEAN BEECH
Fagus sylvatica

HEIGHT 35 INCHES ▲ CONTAINER: CONTAINER: CHINESE XIXING-WARE

OCTOBER 2012

WILLIAM N. VALAVANIS COLLECTION
ROCHESTER, NEW YORK

Narrow Leaf Evergreen Bonsai

The Culture & Training Of Narrow Leaf Evergreen Bonsai

Narrow leaf evergreen bonsai are probably the most popular group of plants trained for bonsai. Although they are evergreen, the colors vary from season to season. The beautiful winter color of junipers, false cypress and Japanese yews provide interest during the cold weather. Likewise the new growth of some junipers, false cypress and Japanese cedars in spring predict the onset of warm weather.

Growing Environment
Generally narrow leaf evergreens can withstand considerable more direct sunlight than deciduous species. Some, however, grow better if provided a bit of shade during the hottest part of summer. Although trees growing in the ground in nature are not rotated, it is important to turn bonsai on the outdoor growing tables to provide even sunlight all around the tree.

Watering
Narrow leaf evergreen bonsai, especially once established, do not require the frequency of watering that deciduous species demand. Newly transplanted bonsai will need to be carefully checked for moisture requirement for the first growing season. It is possible for narrow leaf evergreen species to wilt when under stress or need water. I have seen full grown pines wilt in late spring due to insufficient watering.

Fertilizing
Like deciduous species, undeveloped narrow leaf evergreen bonsai are heavily fertilized with a high nitrogen content fertilizer throughout the growing season to promote vigorous healthy growth to shape and develop a basic bonsai design. In the upstate New York area I begin applying a water soluble fertilizer in May and finish in October. In addition to a high nitrogen fertilizer applied weekly, a monthly feeding of organic fertilizer cakes is used to provide a steady release of slow release nutrients. This mixture of water soluble and organic cakes has produced excellent results as can be seen in the bonsai featured here.

It is thought that late summer or autumn applications of a nitrogen content fertilizer will promote vegetative growth which might be damaged when frosted. However, this is not true if the bonsai has had a constant application of fertilizer throughout the growing season. In fact, the late summer or early autumn application of nitrogen fertilizer will help over wintering and provide an extra boost for spring growth. If the bonsai has not been regularly fertilized during the growing season it is not advised to fertilize after late summer.

After a basic shape has been created and established for a bonsai the nitrogen fertilizer level is reduced to avoid strong vigorous heavy shoots which are unsightly and not desired. This is especially important for narrow leaf evergreens. Only enough fertilizer should be applied to a developed bonsai to keep the specimens alive and healthy.

Soil And Transplanting
Narrow leaf evergreen bonsai prefer a soil mix which is a bit more coarse than deciduous species. An addition of sand, gravel or other hard material is beneficial for these species which like a quick draining soil mix.

Like deciduous species, once the shape of bonsai has been developed the soil mix is changed to a finer size to limit the growth. Since the breakdown of the finer size organic soil reduces the water drainage it is important to carefully monitor transplanting.

Transplanting developing narrow leaf evergreen bonsai should be on a three to five year schedule, however, fast growing trees might be transplanted annually. Although root pruning disturbs growth, it also allows for quicker vigorous growth.

Developed bonsai must be kept healthy so they too must be transplanted, but not as often as developing specimens. Developed narrow leaf evergreen bonsai are not transplanted as often as deciduous species because fast, vigorous thick growth is not desired.

If the soil still drains well and the tree is healthy I generally do not transplant. However, should water begin to slowly drain and health declines the bonsai is transplanted the following spring. The reduced transplanting intervals will promote shorter needles and compact growth. I have had pines and spruce go without transplanting for over ten years and they are still healthy.

Narrow leaf evergreen bonsai can easily withstand a late spring snowfall as long as the temperatures do not drop significantly. It is often best to allow the snow to melt naturally so branches are not mechanically damaged by hands, brushes or brooms.

Moving Heavy Branches On Narrow Leaf Evergreen Bonsai

**Often heavy old branches can be successfully moved to improve the design of a bonsai.
A healthy specimen is necessary before practicing this technique.**

Many years ago I began experimenting with a technique to move heavy branches on healthy narrow leaf evergreen bonsai. Opposite branching is generally undesirable because the positioning causes a static and symmetrically balanced design. Ideally it is best to have branches on different levels for interesting design.

It is best to perform this technique in spring before the new growth begins so the rapid accumulation of new callus tissue will cover the new open wound. I have, however, also tried this during other seasons of the year.

After selecting the branch to lower, cut most of the way through the base into the trunk. A sharp chisel works best for heavy trunks and a rubber mallet works well to drive the tool into the wood. Then, carefully push the chisel and branch down to move the branch into the new desired location.

A small stone works well to insert into the open gap to hold the branch in the new position. A guy wire can also be used to secure the branch. Sometimes I wire the branch to be lowered first before using the chisel so wire can be used to hold the branch. It is a bit difficult to wire a branch which has just been pulled away from the trunk because it is delicate and may break away.

Then fill the open area, rock and all, with cut paste or something to seal the area to keep out air. As the new callus tissue forms it will naturally push the stone out.

A few years ago I also tried this technique on deciduous species with good results. Additional information can be seen on page 86 and a video is located on YouTube at: http://www.youtube.com/watch?v=yGOqHLpk_Ok

In September 2011 Doug McDade and Marc Arpag assisted me in a demonstration where I taught how to lower heavy branches. The demonstration tree was a Dwarf Scots pine container grown by Stephen Kozlowski for over thirty years.

A few branches were first wired before we lowered two branches. Then the remainder of the bonsai was fine wired. A few days later the bonsai was transplanted into a larger bonsai container and a guy wire was added to further refine the design.

Before shaping the bonsai was container grown for over thirty years.

A sharp curved chisel with the concave side facing the branch was used to remove the base of the branch from the trunk. The bottom was not changed so the branch could continue to grow.

All the tools and wire were first prepared before explaining the technique and describing the tree to the audience.

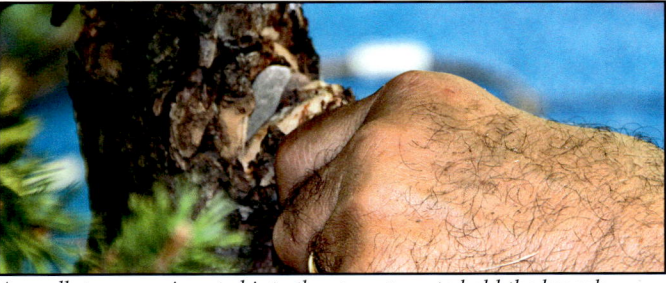

A small stone was inserted into the open space to hold the branch.

After covering the open area and stone with Cut Paste small pieces of bark were pressed into the area to conceal the wound.

After lowering the lowest two branches the entire bonsai was wired to create a more compact form. Additional smaller branches were also split with a chisel to make them easier to bend into ideal positions. The pointed crown of the original tree was removed to create a broad rounded crown characteristic of old mature trees.

Before wiring, shaping and lowering heavy branch with a pointed crown.

After shaping the pine and transplanting into bonsai container.

After lowering the heavy branch, wiring and shaping.

After shaping and transplanting into bonsai container.

Moving Heavy Branches On Larch Bonsai

Although larch is not a narrow leaf evergreen it is a conifer and the same techniques can be applied.

This American larch was collected several years ago and is now established and vigorous. The right branch is growing upward which must be lowered to present an aged feeling.

The front of this bonsai can not be changed. The first branch on the left is growing directly toward the front and must be rotated to the left.

A curved sharp chisel is used to move the branch to be lowered. Use a hammer or rubber mallet to pound the chisel into the trunk, then move downward. Here the chisel got stuck in the trunk and had to be removed before the branch could be lowered and retrieved.

Open and lower branch to new position.

Insert small stone to hold the position.

Apply Cut Paste to seal wound.

Cover with small pieces of bark.

This branch is growing directly toward the front and must be moved to the left.

After using a chisel the branch is put into the new position and held in place with a small stone then covered and sealed with Cut Paste.

The collected American larch after shaping. The first right branch was lowered. The first left branch was rotated to the left and the other branches were wired into the desired positions.

NO. 44 – DWARF AUSTRIAN PINE

Two young container grown grafted plants of Dwarf Austrian pines were purchased in 1969 for $5 each. They were trained for my parents and are named "Mr." and "Mrs." Bonsai. The Mrs. Bonsai featured here developed quicker than the Mr. Bonsai featured next.

This cultivar of Dwarf Austrian pine was originally discovered as a witch's broom growing in Seneca Park, Rochester, New York, in 1932. It grows slowly and has thick dark green needles which are congested and the bark tends to become thick and plated. When trained for bonsai many of the new buds and needles need to be constantly thinned out to allow for air circulation and sunlight to reach the inner sections of the bonsai for new buds to form on the old wood.

Every few years it is necessary to cut back this bonsai to maintain the size and improve air circulation. It is important to remove old needles yearly. In 1991 when Corin Tomlinson apprenticed with me from England one of his projects was to remove the old needles. Since this was the first specimen of Dwarf Austrian pine he worked on he went slowly studying how the tree was shaped. It took him twenty five hours to remove the needles.

This Dwarf Austrian pine bonsai was featured on the cover of the 1993/NO.4 issue of *International BONSAI*. In August 2001 this bonsai received the First Prize Award in the Professional Division of the Midwest Bonsai Exhibit in Chicago, Illinois. It also received the People's Choice Award for outstanding Bonsai Design at the 2002 American Bonsai Society Symposium in Milwaukee, Wisconsin.

May 1977 – *The first potting in a bonsai container.*

May 1981 – *A deeper container was used to encourage growth.*

June 1987 – *Finer development deserved a better container.*

April 1989 – *A more shallow container was used to balance the crown.*

April 1992 – *After old needle removal the bonsai had an open feeling.*

March 2009 – *After cutting back to maintain size the bonsai looks thin.*

NO. 44 – DWARF AUSTRIAN PINE
Pinus nigra 'Hornibrook'

HEIGHT 24 INCHES ▲ CONTAINER: JAPANESE TOKONAME-WARE FROM THE YAMAAKI KILN

MAY 2003

WILLIAM N. VALAVANIS COLLECTION
ROCHESTER, NEW YORK

No. 45 – Dwarf Austrian Pine

This Dwarf Austrian pine bonsai is known as the Mr. Bonsai and is one of two young grafted specimens I started training in 1969. Completely container grown it is easy to look at the developed bonsai today to appreciate the decades which have been lovingly spent in its training.

Like the previous bonsai of the same cultivar, this specimen requires a yearly removable of old needles and thinning out every few years to permit light and air circulation to reach the inner sections of the bonsai. This Dwarf Austrian pine has not been wired for over ten, perhaps fifteen years because it grows so slowly and had an excellent basic shape established twenty five years ago.

The slow needle growth is reflected in the root system as well. It has not been transplanted for over ten years and the water still runs freely from the drainage holes.

This $5 Dwarf Austrian pine bonsai is developing nicely and has never been displayed in an exhibition. I've been holding it for a special occasion and it will make its debut at the International Bonsai Colloquium exhibit featuring some of my finest bonsai creations during the past half century.

September 1985 – *Before removing old needles and thinning out the unnecessary branches on the well established bonsai.*

September 1985 – *After thinning out excess branches, wiring and refining the basic shape. A new container awaits the bonsai in Spring*

October 2000 – *A triangular silhouette has been established for the bonsai which is in need of old needle removal.*

October 2004 – *Note that the silhouette and size have not changed in many years and will remain the same for the next nine years.*

May 2005 – *Heavy surface roots are beginning to become exposed.*

March 2009 – *After thinning branches and old needles.*

NO. 45 – DWARF AUSTRIAN PINE
Pinus nigra 'Hornibrook'

HEIGHT 21 INCHES ▲ CONTAINER: JAPANESE TOKONAME-WARE

OCTOBER 2012

WILLIAM N. VALAVANIS COLLECTION
ROCHESTER, NEW YORK

NO. 46– DWARF SCOTS PINE

Richard A. Fennichia was the horticulturist for the Monroe County Parks Department in Rochester, New York. He was a prolific hybridizer of many species including lilac, azalea, pine and rhododendron. He introduced a select group of Scots pine seedlings which were dwarf with short straight needles which also produced buds on old wood. Many of the trunks suddenly begin to swell and thicken. All of these characteristics are ideal for bonsai training.

I knew Richard Fennichia and purchased many of his Dwarf Scots pines for bonsai training. The largest specimens were growing in large wire baskets and had tremendous trunks and numerous branches. Every one of these large trees died after shaping. However, I also purchased a large number of smaller seedlings growing in six and eight inch pots. All of these younger and more vigorous specimens thrived and many are now well known bonsai.

Well over thirty years ago I sold this bonsai as a young seedling in a small pot to Stephen Kozlowski. He nurtured his bonsai and continued to bring it back to workshops for further development. This bonsai was annually displayed in the Upstate New York Bonsai Exhibition and members watched it grow.

In September 2011 he moved to a smaller home and sold me several of his bonsai, including this Dwarf Scots pine. The second trunk which is too heavy has now created the focal point for the bonsai. In April 2012 I thinned out the dense canopy, wired and transplanted the bonsai for future development.

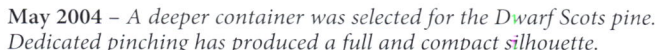

May 1985 – *The second trunk is quite heavy in relationship to the main trunk.*

May 1998 – *The new candles are at the perfect stage for pinching in spring. The second trunk continues to thicken.*

May 2004 – *A deeper container was selected for the Dwarf Scots pine. Dedicated pinching has produced a full and compact silhouette.*

May 2010 – *Short needles have been developed because of the dwarf cultivar and numerous small twigs. The pointed crown looks immature.*

April 2012 – *Many of the branches were thinned out and a few were wired.*

April 2012 – *After thinning and transplanting. Next year fine wiring.*

NO. 46 – DWARF SCOTS PINE
Pinus sylvestris 'R. A. F.'

HEIGHT 27 INCHES ▲ CONTAINER: JAPANESE TOKONAME-WARE

DECEMBER 2012

WILLIAM N. VALAVANIS COLLECTION
ROCHESTER, NEW YORK

no. 47 – Dwarf Scots Pine

This Dwarf Scots pine is from the same group as the previous bonsai. It was sold to Dr. Louis Albright over thirty years ago in a small pot when I was teaching bonsai courses at Cornell University's Plantations. He brought it to class on a regular schedule then slowed his bonsai activities for many years.

Dr. Albright began coming to my studio for workshops several years ago. In April 2009 he brought his Dwarf Scots pine to a workshop where I was pleasantly surprised and impressed with the tree. It needed shaping and I wanted to continue its development into a fine bonsai. Since he was not that interested in this bonsai purchased it from him and even gave him back the Chinese container.

The next day I went to work shaping my new Dwarf Scots pine bonsai which I had not seen for a few decades. I changed the front and did major wiring. Very few branches were removed, most all shortened by wiring.

April 2009 – *Dwarf Scots pine with the previous owner's front.*

April 2009 – *This new front has movement and bends towards the front.*

April 2009 – *The new view of the interesting tapering trunk line.*

April 2009 – *The main branches were all wired before shaping.*

April 2009 – *All the branches were completely wired, before shaping.*

April 2009 – *After shortening branches by wiring. The dead branch was pruned.*

NO. 47 – DWARF SCOTS PINE
Pinus sylvestris 'R. A. F.'

HEIGHT 28 INCHES ▲ CONTAINER: CHINESE XIXING-WARE

JULY 2009

WILLIAM N. VALAVANIS COLLECTION
ROCHESTER, NEW YORK

No. 48 – Scots Pine

In 1970 I visited a local nursery and purchased a small Scots pine in a one gallon can. Although the trunk was not heavy it had movement and several branches which could be shaped in the literati style.

The young pine was pruned, wired, shaped and potted into a round container to emphasize the tall trunk. This species responds well to bonsai training and is winter hardy in our climate.

This Scots pine has been displayed in many exhibitions. In October 2006 I sold this bonsai to Christine Samuel who was developing a fine bonsai collection. She continues to bring her bonsai to me for basic shaping and training. In August 2012 the bonsai was brought to me for a restyling because a branch died. It has also been cut back to maintain the size. This bonsai was displayed in the 2008 1st U. S. National Bonsai Exhibition.

Left
April 1973
A few years after the initial styling the bonsai began to look good in the round container. All the branches were wired and shaped.

Right
May 1978
Continued pinching of the opening candles produced many fine twigs which needed to be wired to create a compact shape.

October 2008 – The wire was removed for the 2008 U. S. National Bonsai Exhibition to show the naturalness of the tree.

August 2012 – The lower left branch died and the tree needs to be restyled and refined.

August 2012 – After trimming back the growth the bonsai was transplanted. Special care must be provided for out of season transplanting.

August 2012 – Old needles were removed and the entire bonsai was wired. Note that the trunk thickness has not changed much in 40 years.

NO. 48 – SCOTS PINE
Pinus sylvestris

HEIGHT 26 INCHES ▲ CONTAINER: JAPANESE TOKONAME-WARE FROM THE SHOUZAN KANESHOU KILN

SEPTEMBER 2006

CHRISTINE SAMUEL COLLECTION
ROCHESTER, NEW YORK

NO. 49 – MUGHO PINE

Mugho pines are not native to North America and must be created as bonsai from nursery stock, rather than from old collected trees which are native in Europe. In late 1995 David Steele purchased two Mugho pines from a garden center and brought them to one of my workshops. After study we made a literati style bonsai from the single trunk tree. He was not interested in the multiple trunk tree so we traded for it.

I created a slanting windswept style bonsai from the Mugho pine and planted it in a shallow round container. It was then wired on two other occasions and in August 2002 it was potted into a custom made Italian bonsai container.

The bonsai continued to grow and had Needle Cast Disease so it was treated and not pinched severly for two seasons. In August 2012 I decided to transplant the bonsai and change the container. Although it is my personal taste to use round containers for windswept style bonsai, my wife suggested a rectangular pot and it looks good. Short needles will now be developed in the future to refine the shape.

March 1996 – *Direct from a garden center before shaping.*

August 2002 – *Before pruning, wiring and shaping.*

August 2002 – *After shaping into a slanting windswept style bonsai.*

July 2003

In April 2003 two handmade containers were purchased for this bonsai, one American and the other Italian. However, neither of them were perfect, although the Italian container was close. Fine quality exhibition containers are currently being designed and manufactured by Certre' S.A.S. in Treviso, Italy. I contacted the proprietor Mario Remeggio with a specific size, design and color for a custom container for my bonsai. Through an unbelievable effort of his artisans and FedEx, the container arrived in Rochester in only three days and in time to be photographed for my 40TH *Anniversary Commemorative Album. The quest for the perfect container was over until August 2012 when the design was slightly changed.*

NO. 49 – MUGHO PINE
Pinus mugho

TOP TO BOTTOM 34 INCHES ▲ CONTAINER: JAPANESE TOKONAME-WARE FROM THE EIRAKU KILN

AUGUST 2012

WILLIAM N. VALAVANIS COLLECTION
ROCHESTER, NEW YORK

NO. 50 – MUGHO PINE

In May 2003 I found two interesting Mugho pines in a garden center which had several trunks. They were nearly identical and growing in two gallon pots. I pruned and wired one specimen in the multiple trunk windswept style and potted it later.

The other Mugho pine was sold to Ken Buell who worked on his tree in one of my workshops. His tree also had many trunks, so he shaped it in the same style. Later he potted his bonsai in a handmade ceramic container which looks like a curved rock. Both bonsai were similar in shape and size.

Unfortunately my Mugho pine bonsai died, but Ken Buell's lived and thrived. He brought it to workshops for further refinement.

In May 2011 Ken Buell sold several of his bonsai at the Upstate New York Bonsai Exhibition and I purchased his Mugho pine. I immediately wired and shaped the tree continuing in the original multiple trunk windswept feeling.

May 2003 – *The initial potting of the multiple mugho pine bonsai.*

May 2011 – *Before wiring and shaping the Mugho pine bonsai.*

NO. 50 – MUGHO PINE
Pinus mugho

HEIGHT 27 INCHES ▲ CONTAINER: AMERICAN, DAVID LOMAN

AUGUST 2011

WILLIAM N. VALAVANIS COLLECTION
ROCHESTER, NEW YORK

no. 51 – Miyajima Japanese Five-needle Pine

The Miyajima cultivar of Japanese five-needle pins has been used for bonsai training for over 350 years in Japan. The bright blue green needles are attractive throughout the bonsai. This cultivar is perfect for bonsai training and can withstand wiring and pruning techniques.

This bonsai began as a young grafted tree and the rough bark of the Japanese black pine understock can be enjoyed at the base of the trunk. After growing in a field to attain the size desired it was lifted and trained in a container for perhaps fifty years before it was imported to the United States.

In May 2011 Ken Buell sold some of his bonsai and Ronald Maggio purchased it upon my recommendation because I saw the potential for a hidden masterpiece. During the summer of 2011 and spring 2012 I wired and shaped the bonsai for Mr. Maggio. This bonsai was displayed in the 2012 3rd U. S. National Bonsai Exhibition.

May 2011 – *Before wiring and shaping.*

no. 51 – Miyajima Japanese Five-needle Pine
Pinus parviflora 'Miyajima'

HEIGHT 16 INCHES, LEFT TO RIGHT 43 INCHES ▲ CONTAINER: CHINESE

JUNE 2012

Ronald Maggio Collection
ROCHESTER, NEW YORK

No. 52 – Tsukasa Nishiki Japanese Black Pine

The Nishiki Japanese black is also known as Cork bark Japanese black pine. The Japanese word "nishiki" means brocade and is used to describe plants with unusual corky bark which does not fall off for many years. There are several species, including Japanese red, Japanese black and Ponderosa pines which also have this characteristic. Several different cultivars of Japanese black pine have corky bark and Tsukasa is among the best. In the early 1960s Yuji Yoshimura introduced this cultivar to America and it is also known as the Yoshimura Clone. He felt this variety was the best Japan had to offer at that time because the thick corky bark begins to develop from the second year after grafting. It has pure white buds rather than reddish buds which indicates increased vigor, since they are not as strong as the common Japanese black pine. Other cultivars take many years to develop rough bark which is not corky.

This cultivar must be propagated by grafting because cuttings will not root. Today there are other cultivars which will easily root. Since it must be grafted, it is important that the union be low so the corky bark develops at the soil level rather than a few inches higher which will present an unstable effect. Grafting in the crown area of seedlings is a bit difficult and time consuming so American nurserymen do not practice this technique.

This Tsukasa nishiki Japanese black pine was grafted by Joseph C. Burke in 1970. He was a skilled propagator, horticulturist as well as bonsai designer who taught me a great deal about how to grow and propagate plants. After searching for many years for the best Nishiki Japanese black pine he finally talked Yuji Yoshimura out of a few scions and he began to graft them.

In 1975 I found Mr. Burke and was able to purchase a specimen in a three gallon pot for training. I allowed the tree to acclimate to Rochester and took a few scions for grafting. After studying the growth habit I learned that this specimen grew the corky bark in straight lines so decided to train the bonsai with straight lines to emphasize the unusual bark and avoid curves which might break the bark. An iron rod was used for several years to shape the bottom trunk.

After establishing the basic form short compact needles were encouraged by cutting back growth and reducing the watering. This bonsai was the logo for the 1989 Magic Bonsai Symposium and was featured in the 1995/NO. 4 issue of *International BONSAI*.

October 1978 – *A large deep bonsai container was the first bonsai container for the Nishiki Japanese black pine bonsai.*

October 1986 – *Before trimming to encourage small needles. After old needles were removed the current season's growth was reduced.*

October 1986 – *After trimming to encourage small needles. The sunlight and removal of needles and new growth will encourage small needles.*

May 2001 – *Compact foliage has now been developed. A smaller new container was selected to emphasize the trunk.*

NO. 52 – TSUKASA NISHIKI JAPANESE BLACK PINE
Pinus thunbergii var. *corticosa* 'Tsukasa'

TOP TO BOTTOM 30 INCHES ▲ CONTAINER: JAPANESE TOKONAME-WARE

APRIL 1993

WILLIAM N. VALAVANIS COLLECTION
ROCHESTER, NEW YORK

The Origin Of Dwarf Plant Cultivars

Dwarf and unusual varieties of plants are highly prized in the horticultural community as being unusual or superior to what is commonly available. With the decreased size of the typical home garden, dwarf plants fit much better into the smaller landscape. They often make excellent plants for bonsai training. Unusual seedlings, bud mutations and witches' brooms are sources for unusual and dwarf plants often trained for bonsai and used in rock gardens.

Japanese horticulturists have been selecting unusual and odd plants for centuries, many of them dwarf in plant character and good for bonsai. All are not, because while some dwarf plants remain small, their foliage might be quite large, or twisted and out of scale for the diminutive plant. Variegated plants were quite popular a couple of hundred years ago in Japan and many old manuals describing these prize plants still exist.

The Japanese use a rather loose term to describe a group of plants as "yatsubusa," which literally means cluster of eight buds and generally means dwarf. In order to be considered as a yatsubusa cultivar plants generally have short internodes, multiple buds, root easy and also have the ability to grow new buds on old wood. Most also have small foliage which can withstand reduced light in tight congested plants. Many of these plants were originally discovered as witches' brooms.

A witches' broom is an abnormal shrub like growth on a tree which can be caused by mutation, insects, virus or diseases. They are mostly found on woody plants, but occasionally on herbaceous plants as well. They look like a compact version of the parent tree because an abnormal number of buds are formed which grow into short branches and have smaller than normal size foliage. The new growth is healthy and grows at a much slower growth rate than the parent tree.

The term witches' broom comes from the German words which mean a broom a witch uses for flying because the dense twigs resemble a broom. They are usually valued in the ornamental horticulture community as a source of unusual and dwarf plant material. There are plant collectors who travel around the country searching for witches' brooms. Some even have blogs describing their discoveries which often become economically valuable. When in college I used to hunt for witches' brooms and was once stopped by a State Trooper when I was half way up a tree taking scions. I still look for them which is not recommended while driving. The Valavanis dwarf cypress, which I did not name, described later originated from a witches' broom I discovered in New Jersey.

Many of the dwarf, including yatsubusa cultivars, of plants originated from witches' brooms. Spruce and pine are two common species which have produced a great number of new dwarf cultivars now popular in the garden landscape as well as for bonsai. Maples, elms, false cypress, ginkgo, cryptomeria, Chinese and flowering quince are species which have yatsubusa cultivars commonly trained for bonsai.

To maintain the original character of the dwarf witches' broom the plant must be asexually or vegetatively propagated usually by grafts or cuttings. Part of the original tissue must be used to create new plants. If the new plant has horticultural merit it will be propagated and named, thus becoming a cultivar of the parent tree.

Witches' brooms often form cones or seed. If viable seed is collected and grown, different seedlings will be found. Sometimes those seedlings produce interesting plants and subsequently become named cultivars. But in order to be a cultivar the plant must be asexually propagated.

Some dwarf conifers which originated from a witches' broom and have been propagated and grown as cultivars have in fact, also formed witches' brooms thus producing new varieties. For example the Birds nest spruce originated a witches' broom on a Norway spruce in Germany and subsequently grew a witches' broom resulting in the popular Little Gem spruce.

It is important to carefully watch seedlings to see how they grow and perhaps differ from the species. Weeping, variegated, upright, rough or smooth bark and other different growth characteristics are often searched for by horticulturists as something new for the garden or bonsai training. Some plants from witches' brooms are too congested with tiny foliage which are useless for the garden and bonsai as well. Satsuki azaleas often grow witches' brooms which are usually pruned off when found.

This witches' broom was recently discovered on the Dwarf Alberta spruce bonsai on the next page. It has tiny straight needles and will be studied. Cuttings will be taken for future propagation and possible introduction.

NO. 53 – DWARF ALBERTA SPRUCE

The Dwarf Alberta spruce is a popular dwarf conifer for the garden landscape and for bonsai. It's easy availability in garden centers has made it a popular tree for people beginning the bonsai hobby.

This introduction of this cultivar to the American nursery industry is interesting. Two prominent horticulturists from the Arnold Arboretum were returning home from southwestern Canada at Lake Laggan, in Alberta Province, in 1904. When they learned their return train home was several hours late they hiked into the nearby woods and found four naturally dwarf trees of Alberta or White spruce, *Picea glauca* var. *Albertiana*. They had a dense conical growth habit and were probably seedlings from a witches' broom. Cuttings were taken, the plant was named Dwarf Alberta spruce, *Picea glauca* 'Conica,' and it is now widely distributed around the globe.

The ease of propagation, dwarf size and conical form has made it abundantly available for landscape, patio planters and topiary use. Recently several dwarf cultivars have been introduced, perhaps from witches' brooms which are slower growing and have interesting color.

Experienced bonsai hobbyists tend to avoid Dwarf Alberta spruce because they have learned that the branches have a poor memory. After wiring the branches return to their previous shape. It is difficult to train this plant with wire, but it can be done. Perhaps wiring every other year will give satisfactory results. If not periodically thinned out the inner branches tend to die out and spider mites quickly invade and turn the short needles an off green or gray color. Periodic spaying with water helps to reduce these pests.

This Dwarf Alberta spruce bonsai was started in a beginner's workshop over thirty years ago when Lucille Miller was studying bonsai with Yuji Yoshimura. It was continually returned to his workshops for over fifteen years for training.

In April 2010 Lucille Miller was reducing her bonsai collection and this large tree was difficult for her to manage. She had it transplanted into a Korean mica pot and was going to sell the bonsai. I immediately recognized a gem in the rough and took her tree to refinement. The front was changed, branches trimmed and an iron bar was used to straighten the top of the trunk. She exhibited the bonsai in the 2010 2ND U. S. National Bonsai Exhibition. At the conclusion of the exhibition I purchased the Dwarf Alberta spruce bonsai for my collection.

Detail view of the witches' broom which developed in the upper right area of the bonsai.

April 2010 – *Before redesigning and repotting this bonsai was growing in a Korean mica pot.*

May 2010 – *After changing the front, trimming and repotting into a Chinese container.*

NO. 53 – DWARF ALBERTA SPRUCE
Picea glauca 'Conica'

HEIGHT 35 INCHES ▲ CONTAINER: CHINESE XIXING-WARE

OCTOBER 2012

WILLIAM N. VALAVANIS COLLECTION
ROCHESTER, NEW YORK

NO. 54 – DWARF ALBERTA SPRUCE

Two tray landscapes of Dwarf Alberta spruce were created by Marianne Tucke at workshops with visiting bonsai artists in April 1974 and May 1975. In April 1976 Marianne Tucke refined the design of her tray landscapes in one of my workshops.

In May 1982 I found a large Japanese bonsai container in California and carried it home. After careful study we decided to combine the two tray landscapes to create a single forest. In May 1982 we combined the two tray landscapes which was effective because individually had been trained for ten years. The trees grew well and the rocks were hidden in the moss. This bonsai has only been trained by pinching part of the growth yearly.

Mrs. and Mr. Tucke retired to South Carolina in 1984 along with her bonsai collection. It it interesting to note that this bonsai continued to thrive in South Carolina, despite the intense heat. The bonsai was first transplanted in 1993.

I had a new idea for this forest bonsai for refining and transplanting so it would be featured in my 40th Anniversary Exhibit. In 2001 I commissioned Brussel Martin, Brussel's Bonsai Nursery, Olive Branch, Mississippi, to handmake a flat stone out of "Ciment Fondue." He added a few extra iron bars in the Ciment Fondue for extra support because the planting is large.

In March 2001 I brought the Dwarf Alberta spruce forest bonsai from South Carolina to Rochester, New York, in preparation for my 40TH Anniversary Bonsai Exhibit which was held in September 2003. In June 2002 I transplanted the bonsai from the container on to the flat rock. Later my wife, Diane, made a plywood base for the rock to avoid breakage of the Ciment Fondue. She used marine grade plywood and used the edge of the flat rock as a cutting guide. Anytime the bonsai was moved we simply carried the bonsai planted on the rock, sitting on the plywood base. Once on display the plywood base was removed. It is interesting to note that the original plywood base lasted nine years and was replaced in 2012 with another base made of pressure treated wood.

Mrs. Tucke later gave me her bonsai collection including this Dwarf Alberta spruce bonsai. Very little wire has been used for this bonsai. Only a few thin guy wires are used to spread the forest. It quickly becomes bushy and periodically the entire foliage must be thinned and branches removed.

Rather than removing all of the trees for transplanting, I simply add new soil to the edges of the planting for maintaining healthy growth.

Originally I was creating a low compact shape, however, I'm now changing the design to create a large open forest with the foliage up high.

April 1982 – *The first original tray landscape.*

April 1982 – *The second original tray landscape.*

May 1982 – *After combining the two tray landscapes.*

August 1993 – *After ten years of development.*

May 2003 – *Many of the branches were thinned out and a few were wired.*

April 2009 – *After thinning and transplanting. Next year fine wiring.*

NO. 54 – DWARF ALBERTA SPRUCE
Picea glauca 'Conica'

HEIGHT 39 INCHES ▲ CONTAINER: AMERICAN, BRUSSEL MARTIN

JUNE 2012

WILLIAM N. VALAVANIS COLLECTION
ROCHESTER, NEW YORK

NO. 55 – DWARF ALBERTA SPRUCE

This bonsai was started as a cutting in the late 1950s and has been container grown and trained since 1961 by one of the founders of the Bonsai Society of Greater New York. His collection was sold and I purchased this Dwarf Alberta Spruce bonsai in 1974.

The front and back views were changed to display a better surface root system and branch lines. In March 1976 the bonsai was drastically pruned, wired and transplanted into the same rectangular container.

In spring 1978 the bonsai was wired again to emphasize two terminals. In February 1980 the branches were again wired, still studying the crown of the bonsai.

This Dwarf Alberta spruce has been displayed in several Upstate New York Bonsai Exhibitions, the 1978 Mid-America Bonsai exhibit in Chicago, Illinois and the 1980 Philadelphia Flower And Garden Show in Philadelphia, Pennsylvania. In 1982 a photo of the bonsai was displayed in the 3RD International Bonsai And Suiseki Exhibition held in Osaka, Japan.

A new oval container was selected for the Dwarf Alberta Spruce bonsai because of the rounded crown. As the years go by I stopped wiring this bonsai, but rather use guy wires to lower branches. One wire is attached to the base of the trunk and proceeds upward to a branch and is secured. Then another wire is added to the newly lowered branch and continues up. This is continued to shape the bonsai so only a single wire is visible.

This bonsai clearly shows antiquity, which is difficult to describe. The entire atmosphere of the bonsai looks old and natural from the silhouette, surface roots, aged bark and trunk. Over sixty years have been spent loving and caring for this old bonsai. Although this bonsai is not a perfect classical bonsai I respect the age and decades of care and training.

September 1964

The bonsai was displayed in a bonsai exhibit sponsored by the Bonsai Society of Greater New York.

May 1976

The bonsai was purchased in 1974 and the front was changed. Every branch has been wired after thinning out the extra foliage.

May 1981 – *The bonsai is beginning to fill out, and many of the branches returned to their original upright positioning. The upper crown is too bushy and does not harmonize with the lower section.*

October 1982 – *A new container was selected to compliment the round silhouette. This is how the bonsai was featured in the 1983/No. 2 issue of* International BONSAI.

NO. 55 – DWARF ALBERTA SPRUCE
Picea glauca 'Conica'

HEIGHT 50 INCHES ▲ CONTAINER: CHINESE XIXING-WARE

OCTOBER 2012

WILLIAM N. VALAVANIS COLLECTION
ROCHESTER, NEW YORK

NO. 56 – DWARF HINOKI CYPRESS

Dwarf hinoki cypress are narrow leaf evergreens popular in landscape and rock gardens. The beautiful dark green foliage contrasts well with the reddish color of the flaky bark. The slow growth also makes it an excellent bonsai subject. There are numerous different cultivars of Dwarf hinoki cypress, which vary primarily because of the foliage or growth pattern.

In 1973 I was teaching bonsai in the Newport News, Virginia, area and stayed with Jane Henley. She had an extensive bonsai collection and added this Dwarf hinoki cypress to her other trees. Advice and suggestions were made when visiting her garden for its shaping.

When Mrs. Henley was no longer able to care for her bonsai Julian R. Adams, Adams' Bonsai, Lynchburg, Virginia purchased many of her specimens. This Dwarf hinoki cypress was among the group. He grew and trained the large size bonsai for over twenty five years.

I saw potential for a masterpiece bonsai and purchased the bonsai from him. After shaping and transplanting it ito a more appropriate container Ronald Maggio added this Dwarf hinoki cypress to his collection.

March 2012 – *Before wiring and shaping.*

NO. 56 – DWARF HINOKI CYPRESS
Chamaecyparis obtusa 'Nana Gracilis'

HEIGHT 32 INCHES ▲ CONTAINER: CHINESE XIXING-WARE

AUGUST 2012

RONALD MAGGIO COLLECTION
ROCHESTER, NEW YORK

No. 57 – Daruma Dwarf Ezo Spruce

Spruce make excellent bonsai. The short needles, many buds and ability to withstand winter hardiness are all attributes for maintaining a bonsai. This easy to care for group of plants can be cultivated in any size. Larger size spruce, often collected from around the world have wonderful trunks which create the focal point of the bonsai.

The Ezo spruce is a popular bonsai subject in Japan were cold temperatures are common during the winter. They cannot be easily grown in tropical regions. It is recommended to collect old spruce specimens for bonsai. If they are not available, you can go to a nursery to find a specimen. In Japan the spruce cultivated for bonsai is Red Ezo spruce, commonly just called Ezo spruce, *Picea glehnii*. Often outside Japan specimens of *Picea jezoensis* are sold for bonsai. Botanically named Black Ezo spruce is never used for bonsai training in Japan because the needles are too large and the foliage is coarse.

Saburo Kato was one of the pioneers of introducing Ezo spruce to the Japanese bonsai community. When I asked his son, Hatsuji Kato, to please show me a Black Ezo spruce bonsai he only laughed and said we do not use that species for bonsai.

Spruce often develop a witches' broom both in the United States and Japan and many of their progeny have been introduced as cultivars for bonsai, dwarf conifer collections or rock gardens. Usually these dwarf cultivars form a small globe of dense short needles. In Japan they are in the "yatsubusa" group.

At one time there were approximately fifty different Dwarf Ezo spruce cultivars in Japan. The specimen featured here Daruma dwarf Ezo spruce was started from a cutting in the early 1970s and has been container grown and trained. I'm sure if allowed to grow freely in the garden it would easily reach four feet across.

Unlike the Dwarf Alberta spruce, Dwarf Ezo spruce can be easily trained for bonsai using wire. I have wired my specimen several times to keep refining the classical bonsai form it shows. Years ago this bonsai was a shohin bonsai because of the size. Now it is a medium size bonsai because of its growth.

October 1990 – *The awkward shaped trunk bend is not visible now.*

September 2004 – *The front was slightly changed to hide the trunk bend.*

June 2006 – *Many days are required to hand pinch every bud in spring.*

May 2007 – *Some of the buds have been pinched, but it takes time.*

May 2009

As the tree matures the branch tips are growing upward. The heavy well balanced surface roots add dignity and stability to the bonsai presentation.

May 2011

The bonsai has been pinched and then transplanted into a fine quality container. But I am still searching for a pot better suited for this bonsai.

NO. 57 – DARUMA DWARF EZO SPRUCE
Picea glehnii 'Daruma'

HEIGHT 16 INCHES ▲ CONTAINER: JAPANESE TOKONAME-WARE FROM THE BIGEI KILN

OCTOBER 2012

WILLIAM N. VALAVANIS COLLECTION
ROCHESTER, NEW YORK

NO. 58 – VALAVANIS DWARF CYPRESS

In 1970 I got lost going to a nursery in New Jersey and got stuck in a rotary traffic circle. While driving around and around trying to escape, I suddenly looked up and discovered a witches' broom on an Atlantic white cedar, also called Atlantic white cypress, *Chamaecyparis thyoides*. Naturally I stopped and climbed to the top of the tree to prune a few branches for cuttings since it had a dense compact growth habit with fine foliage.

I successfully rooted the cuttings and watched how they developed. Many were given away to my students, collectors of rare plants and nurserymen. Some were also sold at bonsai conventions. Many years later I was at the closing auction of Mayfair Nursery in Nichols, New York and I was looking around during the auctioning. Suddenly I heard "Chamaecyparis thyoides 'Valavanis' and looked up to see one of my cuttings being auctioned. Apparently the nurseryman named the plant after me since I introduced it to the horticultural trade.

Hundreds of cutting were taken since it rooted easily. Robert Kretzer, one of my students took my cutting seminar in the early 1970s and rooted a few Valavanis dwarf cypress. In 2010 he moved into a smaller home and I got one of his cuttings he was training. A few weeks later in March 2010 I reshaped the bonsai and transplanted it. The newly shaped bonsai was occasionally pinched and the wire was removed before it cut into the bark.

In July 2012 I wired, reshaped and transplanted the Valavanis dwarf cypress for further refinement.

March 2010 – *Before reshaping the Valavanis dwarf cypress.*

March 2010 – *The bonsai after shaping, only a few branches were cut.*

September 2010 – *After shaping the bonsai it was transplanted.*

June 2012 – *An abundance of new growth provided more branches for shaping.*

July 2012

The bonsai was allowed to grow with only minimal pinching of the crown to give more vigor to the lower branching. A few small pieces of wire were found cutting into the bark.

July 2012

The bonsai was thinned out, wired and shaped for additional refinement. It will be next transplanted into a shallow fine quality Japanese bonsai container.

NO. 58–Valavanis Dwarf Cypress
Chamaecyparis thyoides 'Valavanis'

HEIGHT 24 INCHES ▲ CONTAINER: JAPANESE TOKONAME-WARE

AUGUST 2012

WILLIAM N. VALAVANIS COLLECTION
ROCHESTER, NEW YORK

NO. 59 – SARGENT JUNIPER

The Sargent juniper is one of the best species of junipers for bonsai training. The owner of this bonsai, Joseph Noga is an avid gardener who discovered bonsai over thirty five years ago. Bonsai benches and a greenhouse full of woody cuttings have replaced weedless vegetable gardens and young flower seedlings protected in a greenhouse.

He has been studying with me for over thirty five years and likes to root cuttings, especially Sargents junipers. In the late 1970s he rooted a Sargent juniper, and grew it in a nursery container for shaping into a fine two line cascade style bonsai. He continues to refine and develop the masterpiece. It was displayed in the Outstanding American Bonsai Exhibition sponsored by the National Bonsai Foundation, Inc., at the International Bonsai Congress held in July 1987 in Minneapolis, Minnesota. Photo courtesy from *Outstanding American Bonsai* by Randy Clark and Peter Voynovich, Timber Press, 1989.

July 1987 – *Sargent juniper after ten years of shaping.*

NO. 59 – SARGENT JUNIPER
Juniperus chinensis var. *sargentii* 'Shimpaku'

TOP TO BOTTOM 30 INCHES ▲ CONTAINER: CHINESE XIXING-WARE

OCTOBER 2012

JOSEPH L. NOGA COLLECTION
WINTERVILLE, NORTH CAROLINA

NO. 60 – SARGENT JUNIPER

Sargent juniper is a narrow leaf evergreen which can be trained into nearly every style. Junipers are excellent for training in the literati style because many of the trunks are slender, especially container grown nursery stock.

Each February for the past thirty four years I made an annual Southern Spring Tour where bonsai programs were presented as well as private sessions for bonsai and horticultural organizations. Paul Gross from Rock Hill, South Carolina, had one of the best bonsai collections in the Southeast. Every year I spent two or three days with him working on his bonsai.

Over twenty five years ago I was looking for a pot behind his shed and found this Sargent juniper among weeds. He said those were left overs from a club workshop and not worth working on. However, we worked on two, one of which is here. When he donated his collection to the Bonsai Society of Upstate New York I purchased it at a club auction.

June 2002 – *Before shaping.*

June 2002 – *After wiring and shaping.*

NO. 60 – SARGENT JUNIPER
Juniperus chinensis var. *sargentii* 'Shimpaku'

HEIGHT 27 INCHES ▲ CONTAINER: JAPANESE TOKONAME-WARE

NOVEMBER 2010

WILLIAM N. VALAVANIS COLLECTION

ROCHESTER, NEW YORK

NO. 61 – EASTERN WHITE CEDAR

The Eastern white cedar is a species which likes to grow near water in the northern areas of the country. They are abundant in Canada and often collected for bonsai.

This bonsai was collected by Marc Arpag in 1989 in the northern region of New York state. It was growing in a rock pocket. Originally the tree was three and a half feet in length against a rock, and the current front was facing the sky. Most of the foliage was growing on the long trunk.

After he established vigor, Mr. Arpag trained the Eastern white cedar in the cascade style. He brought it to many of my workshops getting advice and critiques for the future development. When the foliage developed near the base, the entire long trunk was pruned and the tree was redesigned in a small size powerful informal upright style bonsai.

This bonsai has been displayed in many Upstate New York Bonsai Exhibitions and in 2009 received the Members' Choice Award honoring Yuji Yoshimura. It received the ABS North American Award for the finest North American native species award at the 2010 2ND U. S. National Bonsai Exhibition. In September 2010 it received the BCI Award for outstanding bonsai at the North American Bonsai Symposium sponsored by *International BONSAI*.

May 2005 – *First time on display.*   **May 2009** – *A new pot was chosen.*

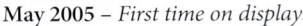

NO. 61– EASTERN WHITE CEDAR
Thuja occidentalis

HEIGHT 12 INCHES ▲ CONTAINER: CHINESE XIXING-WARE

JUNE 2010

MARC ARPAG COLLECTION

ROCHESTER, NEW YORK

NO. 62 – DWARF JAPANESE GARDEN JUNIPER

Dwarf Japanese garden junipers are popular with the large nurseries selling mass produced bonsai to the public. They can, however, be trained into stunning bonsai with the right training techniques and design.

Marc Arpag admired a long Dwarf Japanese garden juniper in a past Upstate New York Bonsai Exhibition and wanted to develop one for his collection. He came to my garden about five years ago and found an old specimen which was over five feet in length growing in a five gallon nursery pot.

After study and cleaning out the old dead foliage he brought the tree to my workshop for advice. Although he originally wanted a long elegant cascade style bonsai, this tree made a finer quality shorter cascade bonsai. It is interesting to note that this bonsai also looks good from the back.

The Dwarf Japanese garden juniper was displayed in the 2012 3rd U. S. National Bonsai Exhibition in Rochester, New York.

May 2009 – *A square container emphasizes the flowing trunk line.*

NO. 62 – EASTERN WHITE CEDAR
Thuja occidentalis

TOP TO BOTTOM 21 INCHES ▲ CONTAINER: CHINESE XIXING-WARE

JUNE 2012

MARC ARPAG COLLECTION

ROCHESTER, NEW YORK

NO. 63 – Rocky Mountain Juniper

Rocky Mountain junipers are abundant in their native habitat in the western United States. They are collected because of the beautiful sculptured dead wood features, not the foliage because it is not ideal for bonsai. The foliage is thin, difficult to compact, light green and has an unpleasant aroma. Therefore the only reason they are collected and used for bonsai is their fantastic and dramatic dead wood areas.

Although you will not find many bonsai in this book which features dead wood, I fell in love with a specimen in April 2005 because of the ancient dead wood focal point. Noted collector Andy Smith, Golden Arrow Bonsai, Deadwood, South Dakota, was selling his collected trees at the Mid-Atlantic Bonsai Festival and this tree was among the ones for sale. I was told by Mr. Smith that the estimated age is approximately eight hundred years old because of the dead wood formation and number of annual rings. It was collected in 2003 and he established a vigorous plant ready for shaping.

I purchased the collected juniper which was approximately six feet across and took it home. It was immediately potted into a large bonsai container at a new angle using a coarse soil mixture to promote vigorous root and foliage growth.

The tree grew well and was transplanted into a large, but more shallow container in 2006. It was never pinched or trimmed as I was establishing a healthy plant which can withstand severe trunk bending.

In June 2008 my assistant, Doug McDade and I compacted the tree. Only one of the two trunks was to be shaped to make certain the techniques would work. First old dead wood not necessary on the six foot long branch was removed using a jig saw. Next a trunk splitter and curved concave pruner tools were used to remove the dead wood the saw could not reach. Only a narrow ribbon of living tissue is necessary. Removing the old dead wood allowed the trunk to be easily bent.

Finally wet raffia was tightly wrapped around the trunk and it was slowly bent. There was one more long branch to be bent. In June 2010 Kunio Kobayashi, Shunka-en Bonsai Museum, Tokyo, Japan, was presenting a demonstration and used this tree to show branch bending techniques. Unfortunately that branch did not live so a new design concept had to be formed.

After considerable thought and many computer generated images I decided to raise the trunk into a standing form. Then the remaining branches were bent into shape. I did not like the foliage of the Rocky Mountain juniper, only the dead wood which required several hundred of years to shape.

The tree was allowed to grow without pinching for two years until June 2012 when I grafted three specimens of Sargent juniper on to the old trunk. Each tree was first pruned, wired then shaped before grafting. In the near future all the old Rocky Mountain juniper foliage will pruned leaving the dark green Sargent juniper foliage.

April 2005 – *The juniper upon arrival before the initial potting.*

April 2005
The juniper was potted with a new planting angle.

June 2008 – *Before bending and shaping the trunk.*

June 2008 – *After bending one of the two trunks to create a new compact shape.*

Bending Heavy Narrow Leaf Evergreen Trunks & Branches

A small jig saw was used to remove most of the dead wood areas. I held the trunk steady while Doug McDade used the jig saw.

A trunk splitter tool was used to remove additional dead wood in the tight areas the jig saw could not reach.

The entire length of the trunk needed to be hollowed out to make it pliable for bending and shaping. The trunk splitter tool came in handy for splitting along the entire long trunk area.

A curved knob cutter tool was finally used to refine the edges so the narrow ribbon of living bark could be easily bent.

The long trunk was completely carved to remove all the dead wood so bending after raffia wrapping would be easy to avoid snapping the trunk and bark.

Slowly and carefully Doug McDade and I bent the raffia wrapped trunk to create a more compact form.

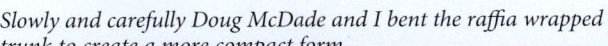

Wet raffia is tightly wrapped around the hollowed out trunk and branches before attempting to bend for shaping.

June 2008 – *The trunk detail after first major shaping to compact and shorten the tree. The right trunk needs to be bent again.*

July 2010 – *In June 2010 Kunio Kobayashi used this tree to demonstrate how to bend a trunk. Unfortunately, the limb did not live and a change was necessary.*

July 2010 – After wiring and shaping the remaining branches the tree was repotted changing the angle to a more upright form. The foliage was not trimmed to allow maximum growth for health and to fill out the basic design now formed.

I was experimenting with the lowest live branch, which can be seen on the right side of the tree. In this photograph it approaches from the back. In the next photograph, July 2010, the branch comes directly in front of the trunk. Later it was completely removed. It is not necessary to make hasty decisions, I often wait years to remove important branches.

Looking at and smelling the tree for eight years, I finally decided to completely change the foliage from Rocky Mountain juniper to Sargent juniper. Using native trees for bonsai is to be encouraged because of their abundance and beautiful forms. However, I have an idealized form in mind and the old foliage does not allow it to become a reality.

It is not widely known that most of the famous Sargent juniper bonsai seen today in Japan have been completely grafted with another cultivar having superior foliage. Thefore, what I am doing is nothing new or different, as it is a common practice in other areas.

In June 2012 I took three healthy one gallon size Sargent juniper and shaped them. The root systems were planted in smaller containers and are concealed in the back. By allowing the roots to remain on the Sargent junipers a quicker and safer technique is used to create a bonsai. After scraping both the young juniper trunk and the ancient juniper trunk the sections were aligned then taped together to keep them from moving and drying out. Finally copper wire was used to tightly hold the two together. Of course afterword the many branches of the Sargent junipers were bent to ideal locations where the foliage is desired.

There is vigorous growth on both the Sargent juniper and Rocky Mountain juniper so some of the old foliage was removed in autumn. The remaining will be carefully studied before removal.

Approach Grafting New Foliage

The foliage of Rocky Mountain juniper is rather thin, light green and has an unpleasant aroma. After careful thought I decided to approach graft Sargents juniper on to the ancient Rocky Mountain juniper bonsai to change the foliage to the compact growing, dark green foliage of Sargent juniper. In June 2012 three one gallon pots of Sargent juniper were wired then approached grafted to the Rocky Mountain juniper. The adjoining bark sections were stripped of bark then carefully aligned and finally wrapped with electrical tape and copper wire ties. The newly grafted Sargent junipers are now vigorously growing and their root systems will be removed in the future.

Sargent junipers before pruning, wiring and shaping.

Sargent junipers for grafting.

Remove the bark where it will touch.

Tie securely to avoid movement.

After grafting avoid pruning old foliage.

NO. 63 – ROCKY MOUNTAIN JUNIPER
Juniperus scopulorum

HEIGHT 33 INCHES ▲ CONTAINER: CHINESE XIXING-WARE

JULY 2010

WILLIAM N. VALAVANIS COLLECTION
ROCHESTER, NEW YORK

Flowering & Fruiting Bonsai

The Culture & Training Of Flowering & Fruiting Bonsai

Flowering and fruiting bonsai add seasonal color to your bonsai garden and displays. The season can be long from the late winter flowering Japanese flowering quince to spring with crabapples, continuing on to summer with developing fruit and concluding with ripe fruit clinging on to bare branches.

The general care for flowering and fruiting species is the same as other types of bonsai, but I have learned that the watering and fertilizing is more important for this group of plants.

Growing Environment
Most flowering and fruiting species will benefit from a full sun exposure all day long. However, there are exceptions, especially when a bonsai is in full flower or fruit because the intense sun may decrease the time of appreciation.

Watering
Perhaps the most important element in cultivating flowering and fruiting species for bonsai is watering. Extra amounts of water will be necessary to form and maintain the blossoms and fruit. Some species, like Wisteria and Porcelain berry benefit from placing in shallow pans of water during the hot weather. Species with large leaves like Chinese quince often wilt during the hot summer months, especially when developing fruit or if pot bound. If transplanting was not performed in spring, it is often beneficial to place the pot bound bonsai in a shallow basin of water during the summer until it can be safely transplanted in spring.

Likewise, if a bonsai is pot bound, I often take a drill and make holes throughout the soil mass to promote water drainage and air circulation in the soil. Avoid hitting thick roots.

Fertilizing
Like other types of bonsai I use a weekly high nitrogen fertilizer application in addition to a monthly addition of organic cakes. I have had excellent results using this technique and get good healthy vigorous growth.

In mid-summer I also add a high Phosphorus content fertilizer to promote the production of flowers and fruit. This is in addition to the other two fertilizers used. There are several brands and formulations available in garden centers. Some of the formulations easily available I have had good success with are N 12 – P 55 – K 6 and N 10 – P 52 – K 17.

Additionally, during the summer I add some SuperThrive and HB 101 when fertilizing, especially for the flowering and fruiting species. I have had success using this method as can be seen in the bonsai throughout this book.

Soil And Transplanting
In addition to my basic soil mix I add Japanese akadama soil, orchid bark or pine bark for flowering and fruiting bonsai.

Some species produce abundantly each year, while others every other year. If bonsai flowers profusely or more importantly produces a large crop of fruit they should be transplanted yearly or every other year.

Long pendulous racemes of fragrant Wisteria flowers creates a beautiful background for enjoying colorful bonsai in the spring bonsai garden.

Selecting Containers For Bonsai

The beauty of colorful flowering and fruiting bonsai require correct color selection.
This information is applicable to deciduous, narrow leaf evergreen, flowering and fruiting species.

There are several factors to consider when selecting a container for bonsai. The three most important being size, shape and color. Then the following need to be considered: season of appreciation, climate and quality.

Size

The bonsai must physically fit into the container. There are several different methods to determine the size of the container. One idea is to simply study the photos of bonsai in books and magazines to see which bonsai look comfortable in their containers. Then take out a ruler and measure the tree and container and see what the proportions are.

The formula I use for selecting the container size for standing styles is: **tree height equals container length & depth.** A bonsai is measured from the base of the trunk to the apex, not the container rim, which can vary considerably since often the tree is raised up on a mound of soil.

For example, if the bonsai is 12" tall then an appropriate container would be 10" long and 2 inches deep, or 9" long and 3" deep or even 11" long and 1" deep. These proportions based on mass feel comfortable and are well balanced.

Flowering and fruiting species need additional moisture so often deeper containers are used. This is important during the flowering and fruit producing seasons.

Developed bonsai are often planted in shallower or smaller containers to restrict the size of the bonsai while undeveloped bonsai are sometimes planted in pots slightly larger to allow the tree to grow a bit faster.

Shape And Design

After the size has been determined then its time to look at the shape and design of the container. First the shape must be selected. Generally the trunk movement must be considered. Bonsai with straight trunk line movements often look best in pots with straight sides (rectangular, shape, equal sided), while bonsai which have trunk movement look good in curved pots (oval, round, equal sided). Usually I use oval containers in my Introductory Bonsai Courses because they seem to fit most bonsai shapes and beginners can't go wrong with the soft oval shape.

Often symmetrical (round and equal sized) containers are used to emphasize the height of the tree while asymmetrical (rectangular and oval) containers are used to highlight the branching.

I prefer to use containers with straight sides because they are considered to be formal and rank higher than deciduous species which are informal and are ranked lower than evergreens. The design of the container is then selected according to the sides, rim, body and feet. Each must be considered.

Color

Unglazed bonsai containers are often used for evergreens which do not change color with the season and present a quiet feeling. Glazed containers are commonly used for deciduous species because they change color throughout the year and are colorful.

The actual color match or contrast is a personal choice, but generally in classical bonsai the main color of the bonsai (foliage, flowers or fruit) should contrast with the container color. Some people like to match the fruit color to the container and often it is sometimes stunning, but also sometimes it is boring. It's a personal viewpoint and the final choice reflects your appreciation and viewpoint of the art.

It is often difficult to have the perfect container for a bonsai. Sometimes I have a container which is slightly too large or slightly too small for the bonsai, but the perfect color or shape. The compromises and difficult decisions must be made. The container can always be changed if not attractive to the owner.

When all else fails, and you are confused, or are not certain, unglazed brown containers are a safe choice.

Season Of Appreciation

Select the season when you want to display or appreciate your bonsai. If you like to enjoy the flowers or fruit, select a color which contrasts with the main color of the container. If deciduous species are to be enjoyed during their dormant season, then unglazed containers are great to highlight the twigs and bark. Often glazed containers are used for displaying deciduous species to add color to the appearance or to highlight the plump color of the buds or changing bark color.

The container size must also be considered when displaying deciduous species. A deciduous bonsai is fuller and massive when in leaf than when there are no leaves on the tree. Therefore a container which might look great during the winter, may seem too small during the summer. A container which looks great during the summertime may seem too large during the winter.

Climate

Horticultural research has discovered that the roots of trees are not as winter hardy as the tops of the plants. Bonsai grown in the northern, colder regions of the world are often planted in deeper containers so the roots have more insulation during the winter. Bonsai grown in tropical areas are sometimes planted in deeper containers so the trees will not dry out or cook in the intense heat.

Quality

The quality of a bonsai container must be considered when selecting pots for bonsai. A bonsai must be respected and treated according to its beauty, age and history. Fine quality old bonsai are generally planted in antique or older pots with patina, while younger bonsai are planted in newer less expensive containers.

It would look strange to see a young bonsai, still in training, in an antique container, just as it would be odd to see an old masterpiece bonsai in a training pot made of mica or plastic. Try to match the tree to the container and your wallet too.

These are just a few of my personal thoughts on selecting the right container for your bonsai. All must be carefully considered to create an aesthetically pleasing and healthy bonsai for your enjoyment.

Using this information I want to select the perfect container for my Shishigashira Japanese maple, for display. Developmental information for this bonsai can be found beginning on page 73.

This crabapple bonsai benefits from a deep container for best flower and fruit production. The blue glaze contrasts well with the white flowers in spring and small red fruit in autumn.

Blue Container
This is the container the bonsai was planted in for the 2010 2ND US National Bonsai Exhibition. The container was handmade by the American bonsai artist and potter Nick Lenz. I like the shape and design of the container, but the color bothers me. The light blue glaze is pleasing, and that is why I selected it for the exhibition, but I personally do not like the small dark specks in the clay and glaze. They are distracting and many American pots have this characteristic. If this pot were a bit larger, it might be better, also different glaze with no specks. A larger more prominent outer rim might look better with this bonsai. This is a personal taste and although the tree was actually planted in this blue pot for the 2010 2ND US National Bonsai Exhibition, I wanted a change.

Brown Container
The brown color and shape of this container are especially good for evergreens. I like the shape of this container for the tree, but it is too small for this Shishigashira Japanese maple. The corners on the rim have cuts which I like and present an informal feeling. The shape of this container is the same as the deep cream rectangular container, only it is shallow.

Green Container
The deep green color of this container is overpowering for this bonsai. The color would be good if the Shishigashira Japanese maple bonsai was displayed in autumn. The bright orange and yellow foliage will sharply contrast with the dark green container. The irregular oval container shape is interesting and I feel it is suitable for this bonsai. If this container was shallower and longer, in a different color it would be perfect.

Deep Cream Rectangular Container
The shape of this container is good, but the size is too deep and massive for the bonsai. I like the incut corners which present an informal pleasing feeling. This cream color is one of my favorites for deciduous species which are often displayed with green foliage during the summer.

Yellow Container
I like unusual pots, species and styles of bonsai. I have had this yellow container for several decades and in the past it was used for a purple flowering Dwarf Korean lilac and Trident maple bonsai. But for this bonsai, I think the size is too small and the thickness of the container sides are too thin for the massive trunk. Also, the container sides are straight and I prefer containers with outer lips for deciduous species.

Deep Cream Oval Container
I like this container but it is still too deep and massive for the Shishigashira Japanese maple bonsai. This container from China is new and of high quality but the color is too bright for this bonsai. I have another container from the same kiln which I aged by rubbing sumi ink and peat muck into the small cracks in the glaze. But this container is too deep and I do not like the straight sides. This container is, however, my second choice.

Shallow Cream Oval Container
The size, color and shape of this container is excellent for the bonsai! The cream glaze is from a special kiln in Japan and is a quiet deeper cream color. This container was handmade by one of my favorite Japanese potters from Tokoname at the Reiho Kiln. Since this is an old developed bonsai I wanted to respect its age using a high quality Japanese container. The container sides are not straight and add to the informal feeling of the total bonsai presentation.

Final Container After Transplanting
After transplanting the Shishigashira Japanese maple from the original blue container into the shallow cream oval container it was time to apply the moss. Several different moss species with fine textures and colors were collected and carefully planted on the soil surface. The mossing process required two hours. Individual pieces of moss were shaped then carefully planted. I planted a small piece of Corsican mint, *Mentha requienii,* on the left side of the trunk base as an accent. The fine texture of the Corsican mint is different than the moss and will attract the viewer's eye to the left side creating more movement to the total design of the bonsai.

no. 64 – Chinese Quince

Chinese quince is an interesting and colorful species for bonsai training. This species can be enjoyed all year around beginning with the small pink flowers in spring, lovely green leaves with exfoliating bark during the summer and autumn brings colorful foliage and interesting fruit. The exfoliating bark adds a delicate pattern to the bonsai design.

This Chinese quince bonsai started as an air layer from a garden tree over thirty five years ago. It was cultivated in a container to strengthen the roots and finally was transplanted into a bonsai container.

There was a large pruning cut on the right side of the trunk where it moves to the left. The taper was not that good. However, I continued to care for the bonsai and today this bonsai displays excellent taper and the large scar has now healed. Time does a great deal for bonsai appreciation.

This bonsai usually produces a large crop of fruit every other year and although some should be removed, I tend to allow all to develop. The fruit are produced at the tips of the branches standing up, which can present an artificial look.

Once the fruit ripens and is kept cool for a couple of months, seed can be easily sown to get additional plants for training. A seedling from this bonsai is featured on page 195.

This bonsai was displayed in the 2008 1ST U. S. National Bonsai Exhibition and also received the First Prize Award in the Professional Division of the 2004 Midwest Bonsai Exhibit.

October 2001 – *The typical autumn foliage colors are orange, red and yellow. Notice the hole in the lower trunk region which I do not like and am promoting additional callus tissue so it disappears.*

May 2002

A larger glazed container was selected to contrast with the pink flowers and yellow fruit.

October 2003

The crown is beginning to become too thick and must be thinned out to maintain the beauty of the bonsai.

April 2004 – *A larger unglazed container was selected for this bonsai, but the container is better suited for narrow leaf evergreen bonsai.*

March 2006 – *The large fruit often persist until springtime when the new shoots begin to open.*

April 2006 – *A new glazed container was selected for this bonsai which is better suited for deciduous, flowering or fruiting bonsai.*

November 2006 – *This season produced several fruit evenly distributed throughout the bonsai. Notice the hole in the lower trunk is closing.*

October 2008 – *The leaves are near the same size and evenly distributed which indicates good cultural and trimming practices.*

April 2010 – *The new shoots are ready for pinching at this stage.*

March 2010 – *New buds often begin swelling in autumn, but will not open until springtime.*

November 2010 – *Too many fruit may weaken the health of the bonsai.*

April 2012

The colorful spring growth this year has not produced any fruit.

November 2012

The excellent trunk taper and fine twig ramification can be appreciated in winter.

NO. 64 – CHINESE QUINCE
Pseudocydonia sinensis

HEIGHT 23 INCHES ▲ CONTAINER: CHINESE

OCTOBER 2012

WILLIAM N. VALAVANIS COLLECTION
ROCHESTER, NEW YORK

no. 65 – Chinese Quince

This Chinese quince is from the same group of air layers as the previous bonsai. They were quite similar in shape so I decided to change the style of this specimen to a cascade bonsai.

The first right branch is quite low and needed to be removed, especially if a cascade style was to be developed. The cascading trunk should be the lowest and there should not be one below.

Rather than pruning the lowest branch I air layered it because it had good movement from training it as a low side branch. The air layer easily rooted and became a shohin bonsai which is featured on page 191.

After the basic form was established the first left branch was allowed to lengthen to create a cascade style. The branch grew to great lengths and was periodically cut back to increase taper and small side branches. When the long branch was developed the bonsai was used as the logo for the Millennium Bonsai Symposium in 2000.

August 1995
Trained from an air layer for approximately thirty five years.

October 1996 – *The autumn color of Chinese quince is spectacular. The first right branch is too low and must be removed.*

July 1999 – *The lowest right branch was air layered, then a branch on the left was allowed to grow to develop a cascade style bonsai.*

January 2007 – *This bonsai usually produces a few fruit each year.*

April 2009 – *The crown is now developed and the lower trunk is next.*

NO. 65 – CHINESE QUINCE
Pseudocydonia sinensis

TOP TO BOTTOM 33 INCHES ▲ CONTAINER: JAPANESE TOKONAME-WARE

APRIL 2012

WILLIAM N. VALAVANIS COLLECTION
ROCHESTER, NEW YORK

NO. 66 – CHINESE QUINCE

This Chinese quince is actually the lowest side branch of the bonsai on the previous page. The tree was developing for a cascade style and this branch was too low.

Since the lowest branch had movement and several twigs from being trained as a side branch I decided to air layer it for a future shohin bonsai.

Early summer is the best time to air layer Chinese quince and they should be well rooted by the end of the summer. When thick fleshy roots are visible through the polyethylene, do not cut the branch being air layered off. It is best to remove some the long-fibered sphagnum moss and add another thin layer over the new brittle roots. The heavy roots will quickly form fine fibrous roots and the branch can be safely removed in about another week.

After removing the new air layered branch plant it into a large deep container to establish a good root system. I left the new plant in the large pot for a few seasons before beginning to train it as a shohin bonsai. The lowest branch on the left was in an awkward position so it was removed. It would have been difficult to train upward and also down for a cascade style bonsai.

This new shohin Chinese quince bonsai is developing nicely and actually can be appreciated from two sides. Therefore I planted it along the center line of the small bonsai container so the tree looks correctly planted from the front as well as the back.

It is interesting that this Chinese quince bonsai usually produces a few fruit but always flowers each spring. When in fruit the tree is often placed in a shallow basin of water during the hot summer weather.

July 1999 – *The Chinese quince is to be trained in the cascade style so the lowest branch on the right side must be removed. It was air layered to create another bonsai.*

July 1999 – *The first heavy coarse roots can be seen. Do not remove the air layer at this time. Add another thin layer of long-fibered sphagnum moss and wait for about a week for fibrous new roots to develop.*

July 1999 – *After cutting off the air layered branch do not remove all of the long-fibered sphagnum moss.*

July 1999 – *The air layered branch was planted in a deep pot for a few seasons. The lowest branch on the left was removed.*

May 2005 – *Shohin Bonsai from the front view in flower.*

January 2007 – *The exfoliating bark can be appreciated during the winter.*

October 2010 – *Shohin bonsai from the back view.*

NO. 66 – CHINESE QUINCE
Pseudocydonia sinensis

HEIGHT 14 INCHES ▲ CONTAINER: CHINESE

OCTOBER 2010

WILLIAM N. VALAVANIS COLLECTION
ROCHESTER, NEW YORK

no. 67 – Chinese Quince

Chinese quince can be easily started from seed which has been kept cold for a few months. The previous two bonsai continually produce fruit and I removed the seed and grew thousands of seedlings starting in 1989. Some were planted in the back field for heavy trunk development and to produce fruit for additional propagation.

Most of the seedlings were first potted in small three inch pots during the first season and many reached two feet in height. During the second year the seedlings were wired for trunk movement. Once the trunks formed movement the wire was removed and they were planted in raised beds to allow for further trunk development.

Many of the seedlings were staked to keep a single main trunk upright. The lower branches were allowed to grow wild as sacrifice branches to form a thicker lower trunk region.

We dug many of the Chinese quince seedlings in 1996 for bonsai training. Robert Blankfield, was digging and purchased one of the small stumps before I could examine it. He continued to bring it to my workshops for training and took excellent care of the plant. We inarch grafted a branch on the left side where one was needed to complete the design.

That Chinese quince was probably one of the best we grew. In 2003 Mr. Blankfield sold several of his bonsai and I was able to purchase his Chinese quince.

I am trying to maintain a small size for this bonsai. In the summer it is sometimes necessary to trim the tree twice a week. It is leaf cut during the summer also to develop small foliage and more delicate twigs.

May 1999 – *Three years after digging from the raised bed.*

January 2000 – *The tree was continually thinned out to form good structure.*

June 2002 – *Several different containers were tested for a perfect fit. Both of these red containers are similar. This container is shallow.*

June 2002 – *This container, of the same design, is deeper. We finally planted the Chinese quince in the shallow container.*

May 2003 – *A rectangular container was also used, but is not perfect.*

July 2003 – *This oval container presents a quiet feeling.*

April 2007 – *A larger container, better suited for narrow leaf evergreens, was tried.*

April 2008 – *A glazed container was finally selected for the Chinese quince bonsai. The vertical lines of the container add to the design.*

April 2010

Each spring this Chinese quince bonsai must be thinned out because of the numerous small leaf buds. It is transplanted every two years in spring. The scar on the lower front trunk is where one of the sacrifice branches grew. It is continually filled in with Cut Paste. An epoxy putty can also be used to fill the hole so new bark can quickly cover the scar.

To date this bonsai has not flowered or fruited. Each spring I carefully inspect the branches hoping to find small flower buds before trimming. In order to prevent leaf burn on this small size bonsai it is placed in 50% shade house in June when and if the hot weather arrives.

NO. 67 – **CHINESE QUINCE**
Pseudocydonia sinensis

HEIGHT 13 INCHES ▲ CONTAINER: CHINESE XIXING-WARE

OCTOBER 2012

WILLIAM N. VALAVANIS COLLECTION
ROCHESTER, NEW YORK

NO. 68 – LAVENDER STAR FLOWER

The Lavender star flower is also commonly known as Crossberry and Star of David. It is native to Africa and I saw several hedges in South Africa in 2011. This species is not winter hardy throughout most of the United States so it must be cultivated indoors during the winter. It adapts to indoor conditions and can be easily grown in a home.

The Lavender star flower produces long shoots with flowers at the terminals so they must be continually trimmed for a good shape and to enjoy the purple flowers during the summer.

This bonsai was originally trained by Lynn Perry, one of my original bonsai teachers. I stood the tree upright and changed the container for balance.

October 2008 – *Original design of the Lavender star flower in a shallow container.*

October 2010 – *The bonsai was redesigned and planted in a deeper container.*

NO. 68 – LAVENDER STAR FLOWER
Grewia occidentalis

HEIGHT 19 INCHES ▲ CONTAINER: JAPANESE

OCTOBER 2012

WILLIAM N. VALAVANIS COLLECTION
ROCHESTER, NEW YORK

NO. 69 – CRABAPPLE

The crabapple is a popular flowering bonsai which also can be enjoyed when in fruit. There are many species and a multitude of different cultivars available. They have been selected for flowers, fruit, growth form as well as disease resistance. Once a crabapple bonsai develops fine twigs, it can be appreciated in winter.

I collected this crabapple from an old abandoned nursery on Long Island near where I went to college. At that time I would take a college buddy with me to do the digging. After finding a suitable specimen it was drastically pruned and I proceeded to the next tree. I paid my friend $5 for each stump he dug. This way more specimens could be collected in a shorter amount of time.

Many crabapples were collected and this one was approximately ten feet tall. I drastically pruned it down to two feet in October 1969 when it was collected. Crabapples are strong and can successfully be collected in autumn, when other species can not. After I brought it home all the field soil was removed and it was planted in a ground bed for a couple of years to develop fine fibrous roots.

Numerous adventitious shoots grew and they were trained for the future branching. The stump was then planted into a wooden box so the new branches could be easily trained. Finally it was planted into a series of round containers to emphasize the long first branch.

The initial area of drastic pruning began to decay many years ago and the old wood was carved away. In 1993 the back section showed evidence of decay. This area now adds a special dimension and mystique to the bonsai design since the "old apple tree" now has a hollowed out trunk. It is interesting to note that this crabapple has two fronts when displayed.

August 1993 – *Main viewing side featuring the tapering trunk.*

August 1993 – *This viewing side features the hollow trunk focal point.*

October 2005 – *The colorful small fruit contrast with the red glazed container. This bonsai flowers every year but does not always set fruit.*

This crabapple bonsai was collected on the same day as the crabapple bonsai I donated to the National Bonsai Foundation, Inc. for the National Collection of North American Bonsai at the National Bonsai and Penjing Museum at the U. S. National Arboretum in Washington, DC.

April 2005 – *The flower buds are pink before they mature to white.*

April 2005 – *The trunk is not watered to avoid filling the hollow section.*

May 2007 – *The well formed surface roots balance the heavy trunk.*

May 2007 – *The heavy canopy is balanced with the massive container.*

October 2012

The fruit are evenly distributed throughout the canopy.

NO. 69 – CRABAPPLE
Malus sp.

HEIGHT 36 INCHES ▲ CONTAINER: CHINESE CANTON-WARE

OCTOBER 2012

WILLIAM N. VALAVANIS COLLECTION
ROCHESTER, NEW YORK

NO. 70 – CRABAPPLE

This small crabapple was used as a training aid when Corin Tomlinson, Greenwood Gardens, Nottingham, England, apprenticed with me. I wanted to teach him about drastic pruning a small container grown deciduous tree for bonsai.

After he topped a crabapple in a four inch plastic pot it was transplanted into a larger pot with a coarser sized soil. He allowed one branch to grow as an escape or sacrifice branch to increase the thickness of the lower trunk. A small size bonsai was then developed, however, I liked the long sacrifice branch and decided to train it as a focal point branch.

This small size crabapple bonsai flowers and fruits every year. The tree is usually evenly covered with small red fruit hanging from the branches.

Originally this bonsai was in a blue gazed rectangular container. When the long branch was developed I wanted to emphasize the length so used a round container. The antique white glazed Japanese container was selected to contrast with the red fruit. However, this crabapple also has white flowers with pink buds and does not provide enough contrast for my taste so a blue glazed container was chosen to provide year around contrast. It is amazing how much difference the color of a container will make on the entire bonsai design.

April 2007 – *This bonsai is attractive from both sides.*

April 2007 – *The small pink buds open to white blossoms.*

May 2007 – *White flowers do not contrast with the white container.*

May 2007 – *This viewing side does not show the original drastic cut.*

April 2009 – *The opening pink buds in spring are delicate.*

May 2009 – *The bonsai looks more massive when in full blossom.*

NO. 70 – CRABAPPLE
Malus sp.

TOP TO BOTTOM 14 INCHES ▲ CONTAINER: CHINESE XIXING-WARE

OCTOBER 2012

WILLIAM N. VALAVANIS COLLECTION
ROCHESTER, NEW YORK

NO. 71 – CHINESE WISTERIA

Wisteria bonsai in blossom are the highlight of any garden in spring. The long fragrant pendulous flowers bring a delicate feeling to the appreciation of flowering bonsai.

This bonsai was found growing in an empty field in North Carolina by Marc Torppa, The Growing Grounds. After obtaining permission from the land owner, he dug it in February 1996 with no fibrous roots, only a few subs near the heavy ten inch root base. Since the wisteria did not have any foliage in February, the thick trunk attracted his keen eye as it grew around and up a tree. The wisteria vines covered three acres.

When he returned home to his nursery, Mr. Torppa potted the wisteria stump into deep nursery pot. It was potted rather deep to keep the heavy trunk from falling over.

The wisteria immediately leafed out the following month and grew vigorously. In February 1998 he potted the wisteria stump into a deep mica training pot.

When I saw the wisteria a few days after he potted it I purchased it because it had a few flower buds. It was brought to Rochester where I inspected the base of the trunk to discover an excellent lower trunk form.

All of the long branches had flower buds and they were wired horizontally. Some of the flower buds were accidently knocked off, but still were plentiful. It was potted on an angle so the long flowers can be better appreciated.

In May 1999 this bonsai was displayed in the Upstate New York Bonsai Exhibition where it received the Members' Choice Award honoring Yuji Yoshimura. It was featured on the cover of the 2004/NO.1 issue of *International BONSAI*.

February 1998 – *The wisteria before purchasing only two years after collecting.*

February 1998 – *After initial potting and shaping of the long branches.*

May 2000

Two years after the initial shaping the wisteria bonsai is developing into a colorful spring flowering bonsai. It is kept in a shallow basin of water during the summer to provide extra water to support the large foliage.

NO. 71 – **CHINESE WISTERIA**
Wisteria sinensis

HEIGHT 39 INCHES, WIDTH 54 INCHES, ROOT BASE 10 INCHES ▲ CONTAINER: CHINESE CANTON-WARE

MAY **1999**

WILLIAM N. VALAVANIS COLLECTION
ROCHESTER, NEW YORK

NO. 72 – CHINESE WISTERIA

This wisteria was started from a common grafted container grown nursery stock. Robert Blankfied noticed an interesting trunk shape of the wisteria in autumn 1995 and purchased the vine. He brought it to my spring workshop for the initial shaping and has continued to develop an excellent form.

Although some flowering bonsai, including wisteria, do not produce annual flowers, this bonsai blossoms dependably almost every spring. Sometime the flowers are hit by a late spring frost, but recover and bloom heavy the following spring. The pot selection is ideal with the delicate Chinese ornaments.

NO. 73 – CHINESE WISTERIA
Wisteria sinensis

HEIGHT 30 INCHES ▲ CONTAINER: CHINESE

APRIL 2010

Robert Blankfield Collection
ROCHESTER, NEW YORK

No. 73 – Pink Japanese Spindle Tree

The euonymus is a group of deciduous or broad leaf evergreen shrubs, trees, vines and ground covers. Many species in Europe, North America and Japan develop interesting fruit which are appreciated by bonsai fanciers.

The fruit of the common Spindle tree is coral colored and unusual. This bonsai, the Pink spindle tree is rather unique because of the large pink fruit. Both varieties have the colorful fleshy fruit covering the small orange seed which is exposed when ripe. Birds like to eat the fruit so the bonsai need to be protected if they are going to be displayed.

This bonsai began as a garden tree which was drastically pruned for bonsai over thirty years ago. The interesting trunk is covered with thick bark which adds drama and impact to the bonsai design. The upper trunk line in the crown is being developed to create a more refined line.

I am still searching for the correct cultivar name for the Pink spindle tree which is one of my favorite bonsai in autumn and is especially colorful for display.

October 2010 – *The colorful leaves hide the thick bark in autumn.*

No. 74 – Pink Japanese Spindle Tree
Euonymus hamiltonianus var. *sieboldiana* cv.

HEIGHT 23 INCHES ▲ CONTAINER: CHINESE

NOVEMBER 2010

WILLIAM N. VALAVANIS COLLECTION

ROCHESTER, NEW YORK

no. 75 – Burning Bush

The Burning bush is a common landscape plant in northern climates because of its extreme winter hardiness and dependable autumn colors. The branches have narrow corky ridges or wings on some of the branches.

This Burning bush was started by Stephen Kozlowski who purchased it in a one gallon pot at a local garden center. It was allowed to grow with an occasional trim and wiring. I purchased the bonsai when he moved into a smaller home. The tree was extensively wired and transplanted into the bright yellow container. The unusual orange and pink fruit are also colorful.

no. 75 – Burning Bush
Euonymus alatus

HEIGHT 29 INCHES ▲ CONTAINER: JAPANESE TOKONAME-WARE FROM THE KOUYOU KILN

OCTOBER 2012

WILLIAM N. VALAVANIS COLLECTION
ROCHESTER, NEW YORK

NO. 76 – JAPANESE SPINDLE TREE

The common Japanese spindle tree is a large shrub or small tree grown for the unusual colored and shaped fruit. There are several different cultivars and seedlings often have varied colors. This species has fleshy fibrous roots which require an abundance of moisture. It is often placed in a shallow basin of water during the summer.

This bonsai was started from a cutting purchased in a one gallon pot in Seattle, Washington, in 1984. During the development of this Japanese spindle tree several different color and shape containers were used. One of the most colorful colors was yellow which provided a vibrant feeling rather than the dark blue quiet impact this container imparts to the viewer.

NO. 76 – JAPANESE SPINDLE TREE
Euonymus hamiltonianus var. *sieboldiana*

HEIGHT 18 INCHES ▲ CONTAINER: CHINESE, CANTON-WARE

OCTOBER 2008

WILLIAM N. VALAVANIS COLLECTION
ROCHESTER, NEW YORK

No. 77 – Dwarf Brush Cherry

The Dwarf brush cherry is an excellent plant for indoor culture. The dark green glossy foliage has white powder puff like flowers which are followed by purple fruit. There are several different cultivars of Brush cherry, some with variegated foliage. The Dwarf brush cherry is slow growing and commonly used in warm areas of the country for topiary, hedges and landscape specimens. The cultivar Teeny Genie grows extremely slow and is often trained for bonsai, but I have had better results from the Dwarf brush cherry.

The Dwarf brush cherry is a broadleaf evergreen, and like most azaleas responds well to drastic pruning for basic trunk shaping. In northern climates where they are overwintered indoors the best time for drastic pruning is summer when the temperature is warm. New shoots will quickly form from old bark and they are easily developed for future branching.

This bonsai was started from a cutting I rooted in 1969 when still attending college on Long Island. I grew it in several different containers and in 1975 a round red glazed American container by Joseph Godwin was purchased from Yuji Yoshimura when studying with him.

In 1976 I used this plant for a demonstration when I returned back to the college to teach a bonsai course. At that time it was much larger, but quickly became shorter after pruning. A seedling was started from one of the purple fruit and it grew taller than the parent plant.

In 1977 a side branch grew fast and needed to be removed to emphasize the slanting trunk line. At that time the right branch was growing upward but was trained into a lower position.

A few years later the bonsai developed and I commissioned Thomas Dimig to handmake a special container for this bonsai. The color, shape, thickness and quality of the container still match the bonsai.

This bonsai is top heavy and fell off the growing table twice. The second time it was tied down but the table top rotted. Each time a new crown was quickly regrown and the tree now has a better taper.

August 1977 – *Before pruning the heavy left branch.*

August 1977 – *The right branch was then lowered for design.*

September 1978 – *The right branch and twigs are quickly developing.*

August 1980 – *Suddenly the trunk is starting to thicken.*

August 1982   August 1986

Sunlight can reach the inner branches after the tree is thinned out.

The bonsai fell off the table and the top was broken and is being redeveloped.

NO. 77 – DWARF BRUSH CHERRY
Eugenia myrtifolia 'Compacta'

HEIGHT 28 INCHES ▲ CONTAINER: AMERICAN, THOMAS DIMIG

AUGUST 2004

WILLIAM N. VALAVANIS COLLECTION
ROCHESTER, NEW YORK

No. 78 – Porcelain Berry

The Porcelain berry is a deciduous herbaceous vine, woody at the base which can be trained as an unusual colorful bonsai for early autumn enjoyment. The berries are spectacular in color changing from pale lilac to yellow and finally to bright blue. The inconspicuous flowers blossom in mid-summer.

Deeply lobed leaves are similar to grape and are often misidentified because the fruit and foliage is somewhat similar The bright green foliage becomes yellow before dropping in autumn. There is a variegated cultivar with pink stems rather than green which are quite colorful, but I have found that it not as vigorous as the common species. Since the vine is herbaceous most of the beautiful delicate thin branching will be lost each year and must be regrown each year which is easily accomplished. Container grown vines can commonly reach three feet in length in only a few weeks. Specimens growing in the ground reach even greater lengths.

This fast growing vine was introduced as an ornamental plant for the landscape in the 1870s. It is so fast growing that it is considered an invasive species and against the law to plant in the ground in certain areas of the country.

The Porcelain berry is rather late to leaf out in spring and it is not uncommon for bonsai to leaf out in late May or early June in the upstate New York area.

Porcelain berries are easy to propagate from stem cuttings or seed. Developing heavy trunks can take years, especially in containers. I have several specimens growing in my garden climbing on a fence or post and appreciate them in early autumn. Each year they are cut back to stumps and allowed to regrow to great lengths the following spring. After a few years heavier trunks will have formed, with flaky bark. It is amazing that trunks appear heavier once potted than when growing in the ground.

Since the long vines need something to cling on, if allowed to grow on their own, will hang down. Shoots will begin to grow upright then when they lengthen their weight will bring lower them.

Often seedlings will self sow and additional plants can be dug from the base of the original plant. When training for a future bonsai, do not trim the vines, allow them to extend as far as possible to increase their girth.

Established bonsai need extra water and benefit from being placed in shallow pans of water during the summer. Also the Porcelain berry seems to attract Japanese beetles.

This specimen was grown by Douglas Taylor who had many growing in his garden for about ten years. Later he gave a specimen to Joe Kennedy who potted it and began to expose the roots. Finally it arrived in my garden and I pruned it back hard and immediately potted it in the display container in April 2008. As the new delicate shoots began to grow they were allowed to lengthen until mid-summer when they were untangled and wired for shape. Neat exhibition quality wiring is not necessary since it will only remain on the plant for a few weeks before it is removed. It is best to simply cut the loose wire off rather than trying to unwind.

April 2008 – *The garden plant which was potted in a training pot was shaped then transplanted into the display container in April. All the new shoots developed in only five months.*

October 2008 – *Like several of my bonsai, this tree can be appreciated from both sides. Early September is the prime time to appreciate Porcelain berry in the upstate New York area.*

NO. 78 – PORCELAIN BERRY
Ampelopsis brevipeduculata

TOP TO BOTTOM 36 INCHES ▲ CONTAINER: CHINESE XIXING-WARE

OCTOBER 2012

WILLIAM N. VALAVANIS COLLECTION
ROCHESTER, NEW YORK

NO. 79 – PORCELAIN BERRY

This Porcelain berry bonsai was started from seed and grown in the ground for five to seven years. It climbed over a post holding a bonsai and was cut back each year. Finally the trunk looked interesting and it was dug for bonsai training.

The plant was bare rooted, and some of the roots looked interesting. Some of the heavy soil was not replaced when potted two years later to create an exposed root style cascade bonsai.

The small size container emphasizes the elegant beauty of the Porcelain berry bonsai, but requires extra watering during the summer.

NO. 79 – PORCELAIN BERRY
Ampelopsis brevipeduculata

TOP TO BOTTOM 26 INCHES ▲ CONTAINER: JAPANESE TOKONAME-WARE FROM THE YAMAAKI KILN

SEPTEMBER 1988

WILLIAM N. VALAVANIS COLLECTION

ROCHESTER, NEW YORK

no. 80 – Tatarian Honeysuckle

There are many species of honeysuckles which have become highly invasive in the northeastern area of the country. They have an interesting bark which sheds in long lengths during the summer. The small white or pink flowers are often sweet smelling and are quickly followed by ripe red fruit produced in pairs.

This Tatarian honeysuckle was discovered and collected by Douglas Taylor who dug it out of a field because of the single interesting trunk. Most honeysuckle have multiple trunks. Large wounds are difficult to cover, so removing extra trunks to create a single trunk bonsai requires many years. After establishing vigor I got the plant and have been training it for over twenty five years.

Small twigs are easy to develop on honeysuckle bonsai, however, they do not live long and must always be replaced by new twigs. It is important to be sure that basal shoots or suckers not develop because they will quickly spoil the beautiful form.

May 2010

Beautiful yellow and white delicate flowers cover the bonsai in May.

no. 80 – Tatarian Honeysuckle
Lonicera tatarica

HEIGHT 30 INCHES ▲ CONTAINER: CHINESE XIXING-WARE

JUNE 2006

William N. Valavanis Collection
ROCHESTER, NEW YORK

NO. 81 – LITTLE GEM DWARF GARDENIA

Gardenias are a well known for their sweet aroma and dark green glossy leaves. This southern plant must be grown indoors in cold climates. The flowers open pure white in color and as mature become golden yellow. This cultivar, which is also known as Daruma in Japan, has single flowers and the habit of forming interesting upright orange fruit which persist all winter long and are full of seed which can be easily sown.

The bonsai was started from a cutting grown in Florida in a three gallon pot. It had a single trunk with interesting structure and a heavy surface root region. I began shaping it in 2007 and keep it in a cold greenhouse during the long cold winter. It blossoms in May filling the greenhouse with its fragrance.

NO. 81 – LITTLE GEM DWARF GARDENIA
Gardenia jasminoides 'Little Gem' ('Daruma')

HEIGHT 15 INCHES ▲ CONTAINER: CHINESE

MAY 2011

WILLIAM N. VALAVANIS COLLECTION
ROCHESTER, NEW YORK

NO. 82 – TOYO NISHIKI JAPANESE FLOWERING QUINCE

In Japan the most popular cultivar of Japanese flowering quince is Toyo Nishiki, because of the multi colored blossoms. This is a vigorous cultivar which can easily reach heights of six feet.

It is easy to locate this cultivar in the United States, but usually the plants will only produce white and pink flowers, rarely red. My specimen has three branches which have red flowers. Several years ago I was carefully looking at it and discovered the three branches have been indeed grafted on. During my visits to Japan I now notice many of the Toyo Nishiki Japanese flowering quince bonsai have been grafted with red flowering branches.

This bonsai consistently produces a large crop of small size yellow fragrant fruit.

May 2011 – *Back view.*

May 2011 – *Front view.*

NO. 82 – TOYO NISHIKI JAPANESE FLOWERING QUINCE
Chaenomeles speciosa 'Toyo Nishiki'

HEIGHT 17 INCHES ▲ CONTAINER: JAPANESE TOKONAME-WARE FROM THE HATTORI KILN

OCTOBER 2000

WILLIAM N. VALAVANIS COLLECTION
ROCHESTER, NEW YORK

NO. 83 – NIPPON DAISY CHRYSANTHEMUM

The Nippon daisy chrysanthemum, also called Montauk daisy, is an unusual species for bonsai. This perennial is native to the seashores of Japan and an excellent garden plant. The succulent foliage presents a striking contrast to the old trunk. Large white "daisy like" flowers are produced in late autumn.

This bonsai is originally from Yuji Yoshimura who imported it from Japan in the early 1960s. His father Toshiji Yoshimura, started the cutting in the 1950s. When Yuji Yoshimura retired in 1995 he had a large auction where I purchased this bonsai. At that time it had three trunks. I cut it back to create a compact shape and transplanted it into an unusual, antique and valuable Japanese container, also originally from Yuji Yoshimura. When transplanting I removed the lowest trunk on the left to create a cascade bonsai. It is the next featured bonsai.

This bonsai received the First Prize Award First Prize in the Professional Division of the 2007 Midwest Bonsai Exhibit in Chicago, Illinois.

October 1994 – *Yuji Yoshimura with his display of Taiwan reed and the Nippon daisy chrysanthemum at an exhibit at the New York Botanical Garden.*

August 2006 – *The Nippon daisy chrysanthemum is repetitively cut back until August so the flower buds are not removed.*

NO. 83 – NIPPON DAISY CHRYSANTHEMUM
Chrysanthemum nipponicum

HEIGHT 27 INCHES ▲ CONTAINER: JAPANESE, SANSHU ICHIYOU

OCTOBER 2007

WILLIAM N. VALAVANIS COLLECTION
ROCHESTER, NEW YORK

NO. 84 – NIPPON DAISY CHRYSANTHEMUM

This Nippon daisy chrysanthemum was originally started from a cutting in the 1950s by Toshiji Yoshimura, Kofuen Bonsai Garden, Tokyo, Japan. His son, Yuji Yoshimura, imported it in the early 1960s.

I purchased the bonsai at Yuji Yoshimura's retirement auction in 1995. When transplanting the three trunk bonsai I removed the lowest left trunk because the others would make a more powerful twin trunk bonsai. I simply divided the trunk by carefully pulling it apart. It had several exposed roots, which I allowed to remain because they were interesting.

The new cascade style bonsai grew well and later I removed a small branch which originated from one of the exposed roots. It too is now a cascade bonsai. Although the flower stems are long, it is important to respect the nature of the species being trained for bonsai and to work with its characteristics.

October 1994
When purchased at Yoshimura's retirement auction in 1995 the bonsai had three trunks. This cascade was created from the lowest left branch.

NO. 84 – NIPPON DAISY CHRYSANTHEMUM
Chrysanthemum nipponicum

TOP TO BOTTOM 21 INCHES ▲ CONTAINER: CHINESE XIXING-WARE

OCTOBER 2012

WILLIAM N. VALAVANIS COLLECTION
ROCHESTER, NEW YORK

NO. 85 – WASHINGTON HAWTHORN

The Washington hawthorn is a species for all seasons with delicate clustered flowers in spring which are followed by dainty leaves and ripening fruit. The autumn color is beautiful with the small red fruit which persist throughout the winter season on bare branches.

This bonsai was purchased from me by Stephen Kozlowski during classes around 1975. He worked his bonsai during several workshops for over thirty years.

When Mr. Kozlowski moved into a smaller home I purchased the Washington Hawthorn and refined the design before transplanting. The smaller, but deeper new container better balances the new compact design I created.

April 2012 – *Original open design feeling.*

April 2012 – *A compact design was created.*

NO. 85 – WASHINGTON HAWTHORN
Crataegus phaenopyrum

HEIGHT 32 INCHES ▲ CONTAINER: JAPANESE TOKONAME-WARE FROM THE KOYO KILN

OCTOBER 2012

WILLIAM N. VALAVANIS COLLECTION
ROCHESTER, NEW YORK

NO. 86 – ROCK COTONEASTER

There are many species of cotoneasters, some are low ground covers while others are small trees. For bonsai training species and cultivars with small flowers and fruit are considered to be best. The Rock cotoneaster is a low growing shrub with small fruit. Small leaf cotoneaster, *Cotoneaster microphylla* and Cranberry cotoneaster, *Cotoneaster apiculata,* are two species which are commonly grown for bonsai.

The Rock cotoneaster has a horizontal growth habit which makes it a good groundcover in the landscape and also a cascade bonsai specimen. The flowers and fruit are arranged as a spray which is quite attractive.

This bonsai was started from common multiple trunk nursery stock found at a garden center. Cora Goldsworth worked on it during one of my workshops in the early 1980s. When designing a bonsai, most students want a single powerful trunk. However there is beauty with slender delicate trunks. Each species must be considered when designing the basic form.

Cotoneasters generally do not form single trunks, but rather a clump of smaller stems. We looked at the base to find the surface roots of each trunk and discovered that they were all connected underground by a single horizontal trunk. Rather than cut away several trunks to emphasize the beauty of a single specimen, a sinuous style bonsai was developed.

Sinuous style forests are favored to those composed of individual specimens because of the care, however they require more time to develop.

A few trunks of the Rock cotoneaster were eliminated and the original positions of the others were moved to form a well designed forest. Some of the trunks, although connected to a larger one, were able to be repositioned for design.

The original horizontal trunk, now thirty years later is visible on the soil surface. A shallow light blue glazed container was selected to emphasize the trunk size and the short cloud shaped feet emphasize the thin delicate trunks.

October 2007 – *The small fruit slowly become red as they ripen.*

November 2007 – *Autumn coloring varies according to the season.*

December 2007 – *Small berries persist throughout the winter.*

November 2011 – *Sometimes autumn coloring becomes red.*

NO. 86 – ROCK COTONEASTER
Cotoneaster horizontalis

HEIGHT 24 INCHES ▲ CONTAINER: JAPANESE TOKONAME-WARE FROM THE TOUSHO KILN

OCTOBER 2012

WILLIAM N. VALAVANIS COLLECTION
ROCHESTER, NEW YORK

no. 87 – Smoke Tree

The Smoke tree is considered to be an old fashioned large multi stemmed shrub for landscapes. Currently there are numerous cultivars selected for different colored flowers or foliage.

In 1975 Harvey Carapella found this Smoke tree as a neglected nursery stock grown in a two gallon pot. He purchased it for $1 and discovered that the original trunk had died and was replaced by several new shoots. The tree was repotted into better soil and allowed to grow.

The new shoots were allowed to grow around the dead trunk section. He brought the potted shrub to my workshop and we discussed the future design of the Smoke tree. The tree began to fill out with Mr. Carapella's care and finally a beautiful bonsai was formed.

The Smoke tree is naturally a multi stemmed shrub. New basal shoots grow and develop into trunks and the old ones die and wither. Although the Smoke tree bonsai was quite healthy and produced a multitude of small beige smoke like flowers the upper trunk died.

Again he brought the Smoke tree back to a workshop and the tree was allowed to grow to see what would develop. Finally we decided to create a cascade style bonsai from the single living lower branch.

This smoke tree was featured in the 1986/NO. 1 issue of *International BONSAI* and received the Bonsai Clubs International Award of Excellence selected by the Japanese bonsai artist Yasuo Mitsuya.

May 1980 – *The bonsai was created from a stump with a few branches.*

October 1988 – *Autumn colors are yellow and orange.*

May 2011 – *After the top died a new cascade design was created.*

May 2012 – *A new blue container contrasts with the opening flowers.*

NO. 87 – SMOKE TREE
Cotinus coggygria

HEIGHT 26 INCHES ▲ CONTAINER: JAPANESE TOKONAME-WARE FROM THE REIHO KILN

JUNE 1985

HARVEY B. CARAPELLA COLLECTION
ROCHESTER, NEW YORK

NO. 88 – RUBY CHINESE FRINGE FLOWER

The Fringe flower is a relatively new introduction to the American nursery industry. Originally from China and Japan, this plant is from the Witch hazel family. Delicate flowers are freely produced in spring, and often extend throughout the summer.

This fast and easy to grow plant is not winter hardy in cold areas of the country and must be grown indoors during the winter. It is heat tolerant when grown in the landscape. There have been numerous cultivars selected for flower color, form and growth habit.

I purchased this Fringe flower from Randy Clark, The Bonsai Learning Center, Charlotte, North Carolina, growing in a three gallon pot. It was grown for a year to see if I could keep it alive in Rochester before shaping.

March 2005 – *Pink flowers in spring.*

January 2006 – *Before shaping.*

NO. 88 – RUBY CHINESE FRINGE FLOWER
Loropetalum chinense 'Ruby'

HEIGHT 26 INCHES ▲ CONTAINER: CHINESE

MARCH 2006

WILLIAM N. VALAVANIS COLLECTION
ROCHESTER, NEW YORK

NO. 89 – JAPANESE WITCH HAZEL

Witch hazel are not commonly trained for bonsai because of their short blossoming period. They are tall multi stemmed shrubs. There are three species of Witch hazel, Chinese, Japanese and American which are cultivated for their spider like spicy flowers. They have been extensively hybridized for superior flowers.

The Chinese and Japanese species flower in spring, while the native American witch hazel blossoms in autumn when flowers are rare in the landscape as well as in the bonsai garden.

I participate in GardenScape, Rochester's flower and Garden show which is held in March to feature spring garden designs and spring flowering plants. Each year I design award winning gardens highlighting the beauty of my bonsai.

Flowering plants are a requirement for the garden so I am always on the lookout for early spring blossoming species which can be created as bonsai. Both Chinese fringe flower and Witch hazel have proved reliable blossom producers when forced in a greenhouse.

NO. 89 – JAPANESE WITCH HAZEL
Hamamelis japoinca

HEIGHT 22 INCHES ▲ CONTAINER: CHINESE

FEBRUARY 2006

WILLIAM N. VALAVANIS COLLECTION
ROCHESTER, NEW YORK

No. 90 – Robinson Dwarf Contorted Pear

This is a rare and little known cultivar of the popular Bradford pear which is extensively used for street trees and in the landscape. The small twigs on this cultivar are contorted which adds interest to the winter silhouette. In 1983 I selected several ten year old field grown specimens propagated by budding from the Shadow Nursery in Winchester, Tennessee, because of the thick trunks and a few lower branches. They were pruned back to two feet, dug, bare rooted and shipped to my studio.

The plants were again selectively pruned to approximately eighteen inches leaving only stumps. As they began to leaf out each new shoot was wired into position for design. Later they were potted into the appropriate bonsai containers.

The Robinson dwarf contorted pear is an exciting cultivar for bonsai because the small flowers can be enjoyed in spring, brilliant orange color in autumn and lovely round fruit during the winter season when the foliage drops.

March 1983 – *The bonsai was created from a stump and a few branches.*

March 1986 – *Small double white flowers cover the bonsai in spring.*

April 2006 – *The trunk is beginning to thicken and develop aged bark and the branching is improving.*

May 2012 – *A main branch became over thick and the bonsai needs to be redesigned. Guy wires are being used to lower branches.*

NO. 90 – ROBINSON DWARF CONTORTED PEAR
Pyrus calleryana 'Robinson'

HEIGHT 25 INCHES ▲ CONTAINER: JAPANESE TOKONAME-WARE FROM THE REIHO KILN

NOVEMBER 2006

WILLIAM N. VALAVANIS COLLECTION
ROCHESTER, NEW YORK

NO. 91 – MIMOSA SILK FLOWER

The Mimosa or Silk tree is a small deciduous tree, native to the United States which is often used as an ornamental in the landscape. In southern areas this species is often considered a weed tree because of quick growing seedlings.

This bonsai was originally collected in South Carolina by Ken Duncan and container grown for several years. The ten year old tree was trained in several different sizes and colors of bonsai containers, but I finally decided on the lovely green glazed Chinese pot. For the past fifteen years the bonsai has blossomed in August and September in the Upstate New York region, while further south they begin flowering in June.

In the evening the leaves often fold up for the night time. The individual flowers do not last long, but there are plenty and always present a colorful display.

NO. 91 – MIMOSA SILK FLOWER
Albizia julibrissin

TOP TO BOTTOM 28 INCHES ▲ CONTAINER: CHINESE

MARCH 2005

WILLIAM N. VALAVANIS COLLECTION
ROCHESTER, NEW YORK

NO. 92 – BOSTON IVY

Boston ivy is a vigorous, woody deciduous vine extensively used as a covering for brick and stone buildings. The plant climbs using small tendrils and is covered with deep green glossy foliage during the growing season. In autumn Boston ivy becomes brilliant red and buildings may seem to be on fire from a distance.

Upon close examination heavy trunks are often found near the bases of larger trees. They can be successfully drastically pruned back to a stump and be trained for bonsai.

This nursery grown specimen was a lucky find. I had it in the blue glazed container for years. The Bonsai Society of Upstate New York had a commemorative square unglazed brown container made to celebrate the 35TH anniversary so I planted this Boston ivy in the container to present a quiet autumn picture with the red leaves. The green foliage also looks great with the brown container as well during the summertime.

October 2005

Brilliant red foliage covers the entire bonsai in autumn.

NO. 92 – BOSTON IVY
Parthenocissus tricuspidata

TOP TO BOTTOM 18 INCHES ▲ CONTAINER: JAPANESE

JUNE 2005

WILLIAM N. VALAVANIS COLLECTION
ROCHESTER, NEW YORK

SHOHIN BONSAI

The Popularity of Shohin Bonsai

Shohin bonsai are the jewels of the bonsai world. The Japanese have always loved small items so it is not surprising that the development of the smaller size shohin bonsai began.

Shohin bonsai are styled the same as larger size trees, however, it is difficult to obtain identical refinement because of their size. The shaping techniques for shohin bonsai are also the same, but more delicate work is necessary. An excellent small size bonsai can have the same impact and grandeur as larger trees. Throughout the world Shohin bonsai exhibitions, organizations and conventions are held because of their popularity.

Shohin bonsai require more care than larger trees because of their size. Probably watering is the most important factor which must be mastered when cultivating small size bonsai.

Often more frequent transplanting is necessary because of the limited soil in the containers. Small containers tend to heat up quicker than larger pots requiring shade in some situations. The soil particle size is smaller than common size bonsai, which although may hold more water, require more frequent waterings, especially during the hot summers.

Species with small foliage and close internodes are better for shohin bonsai training than those with huge foliage and having a coarse plant character. People with limited space find shohin bonsai ideal because they can maintain many different species in various styles in a small area. Maximum winter protection must be provided for shohin bonsai because of the limited soil and small plants.

Count Yorinaga Matsudaira and his wife, Akiko, preparing to take some of their shohin bonsai on a trip. The carrying baskets were made to transport some of their favorite bonsai when they went traveling. It is believed that he began and encouraged the shohin bonsai boom in Japan beginning after 1923.

The Matsudaira Shohin Bonsai Collection

**Count Yorinaga Matsudaira was a pioneer and collector of shohin bonsai.
His efforts to promote shohin bonsai are now enjoyed by people around the world.**

Count Yorinaga Matsudaira (December 10, 1874 - September 13, 1944) began to collect shohin bonsai, called "mame bonsai" at that time, after the Great Kanto Earthquake in 1923. He was a member of the House of Peers from 1909 to his death, except from 1911 - 1914. In 1933 he became Vice-president of the House of Peers. Bonsai was his passion and he was experimenting to see how small a bonsai could be created and maintained healthy. When he was stationed in Nanjing, China, he brought back small trees for training as shohin bonsai.

Count Matsudaira popularized small size bonsai and was the first honorary President of the Kokufu Bonsai Society, which became the Nippon Bonsai Association in 1965. He worked with Norio Kobayashi, a prolific author and publisher, to establish the Kokufu Bonsai Society which sponsored the Kokufu Bonsai Exhibition, starting twice yearly in 1934.

Together with his wife, Akiko, they assembled the largest shohin bonsai collection in Japan reaching one thousand trees. During World War II, most were lost, but about two hundred survived. After the passing of Count Matsudaira in 1944 during the war, his wife maintained the two hundred remaining shohin bonsai at her home in Atami. She was one of the first women in Japan to create bonsai and was assisted by the Kofu-en Bonsai Garden in Tokyo, operated by the Toshiji Yoshimura family.

In 1975 The Nippon Bonsai Association published the deluxe book *The Matsudaira Shohin Bonsai Collection Album* featuring her collection of shohin bonsai, antique containers, display tables and small size display alcove. Photographs of her homes and Ritsurin Park in Takamatsu, Japan, the ancient home of Yorishige Matsudaira's family, were also included in the book.

Akiko Matsudaira passed away in 1976 and her collection was dispersed. Many were sold through established bonsai dealers and occasionally they are displayed. At the 2011 Asia Pacific Bonsai & Suiseki Convention, held in Takamatsu, Japan, six shohin bonsai from her collection were in a special exhibit in Tamamo Castle.

Akiko Matsudaira at her home in Atami, Japan, where she cared for her shohin bonsai. Notice the small pieces of bamboo sticks around the small containers preventing wind damage to the delicate trees.

Count Yorinaga and Akiko Matsudaira next to their shohin bonsai display at the 1st Kokufu ten Bonsai Exhibition in 1934. A Matsudaira Shohin Bonsai Collection display was part of every Kokufu ten Bonsai Exhibition until Mrs. Matsudaira's death in 1976.

Count Yorinaga and Akiko Matsudaira had nearly one thousand shohin bonsai in their collection which were kept on wooden tables. The legs of each table were sitting in a shallow basin of water with a few drops of insecticide to prevent pests from climbing onto the wooden table tops.

no. 93 – Japanese Maple

I was privileged and fortunate to be able to add this Japanese maple to my bonsai collection in 1985. This historic bonsai from the Matsudaira Shohin Bonsai Collection clearly shows antiquity as well as a refined beauty.

For twenty years I tenderly cared for this bonsai and was actually acting as a curator, attempting to maintain the Japanese maple in the shape as I obtained it. The bonsai thrived, but while caring for the bonsai every day I saw a new dynamic line which interested me, but resisted changing the design.

In 2005 I decided to redesign the Japanese maple by changing the planting angle and by inarch grafting branches and a new upper trunk. The bonsai was grafted yearly until 2010.

Looking back at the old historic photos I suddenly discovered that my "new" design is actually the shape that Count Matsudaira created last century. I have enjoyed training this Japanese maple in the spirit of Count and Akiko Matsudaira and feel honored to be able to maintain this bonsai so future generations can enjoy its beauty.

April 1973 – *Photo from the 1973 Kofu-en Bonsai Garden Album of the Matsudaira Bonsai Collection. Height: 4.72 inches.*

The Matsudaira Shohin Bonsai Collection display at the 49TH Kokufu Ten Bonsai Exhibition in 1974 featuring Japanese cryptomeria, Japanese maple, Japanese flowering apricot, Rock cotoneaster and Chojubai dwarf Japanese flowering quince. The Japanese maple is now part of my bonsai collection. It might also have been displayed in prior Kokufu ten Bonsai Exhibitions as well.

February 1985 – *The Japanese maple shohin bonsai as obtained. I could not afford the antique shallow container, but did not think it was suitable for the design. Note the change of planting angle from the original design on the left in the red circle as displayed in the 1974 Kokufu ten Bonsai Exhibition.*

The extremely heavy bulbous trunk base probably developed because it was maintained in a small container for decades. Perhaps the deep container was hiding the base and the lack of surface roots. I planted it in a larger container to establish vigor and to develop more twig ramification for the design.

The bonsai was rotated and the first branch on the right is now a back branch. Therefore the tree needed a new first right branch. The long trunk was eventually shortened and a new top was inarch grafted to return the beauty of this Japanese maple shohin bonsai to the original design Count Matsudaira created.

January 1998 – *Fine twigs are beginning to develop.*

June 1988 – *The small foliage is beginning to develop.*

April 2007 – *After inarch grafting branches and new top.*

April 2008 – *After inarch grafting additional branching.*

April 2007
A sharp drill bit is used to make a hole all the way through the trunk for the long branch.

The new branch was developed from the small bud.

April 2008 – *Several branches were inarch grafted in April. The long branches below were developed the prior year by allowing several new shoots to grow untrimmed. The pink ribbons are to remind me not to trim the grafted branch which is sometimes difficult to see when in leaf.*

235

May 2009 – *After spring trimming and lowering first right branch with a guy wire. A single branch was later allowed to lengthen for the remaining summer to provide another needed branch.*

April 2009 – *Spring growth before pruning. The tree was allowed to grow untrimmed for the entire growing system to provide options for additional inarch grafting of new branches.*

April 2010

The last branch was inarch grafted in April as can be seen in photo. The remaining bonsai was continually trimmed to maintain the compact shape and small foliage.

NO. 93 – JAPANESE MAPLE
Acer palmatum

HEIGHT 10 INCHES ▲ CONTAINER: JAPANESE TOKONAME-WARE FROM THE REIHO KILN

OCTOBER 2012

WILLIAM N. VALAVANIS COLLECTION
ROCHESTER, NEW YORK

NO. 94 – CHOJUBAI DWARF JAPANESE FLOWERING QUINCE

There are many cultivars of Dwarf Japanese flowering quince. Most have been selected for their flowers and plant character. The Japanese word "chojubai" means "long life apricot" because this cultivar has small flowers similar in shape to the Japanese flowering apricot, are long lasting and have rough bark. Usually Chojubai dwarf Japanese flowering quince begins to blossom in early autumn and continues throughout the winter in warmer climates. It is not unusual to appreciate small fruit on flowering plants. This bonsai was started from a small stem cutting taken in 1975 and has been completely container grown. Specimens grown in the ground often have thicker trunks, but usually not refined shapes.

August 1993

The fragrant small yellow fruit adds color to the design.

NO. 94– CHOJUBAI DWARF JAPANESE FLOWERING QUINCE
Chaenomeles japonica 'Chojubai'

HEIGHT 8 INCHES ▲ CONTAINER: JAPANESE TOKONAME-WARE FROM THE KOYO KILN

MAY 2003

WILLIAM N. VALAVANIS COLLECTION
ROCHESTER, NEW YORK

NO. 95 – CHOJUBAI DWARF JAPANESE FLOWERING QUINCE

This Chojubai dwarf Japanese flowering quince was started from a rooted stem cutting taken in 1975. The container grown plant had an unusual root formation so I created an exposed root style bonsai and had the tree planted in a small container. My assistant Brenta Sullivan was making ceramic pots which look like curved rocks and custom made a pot for this bonsai.

The tree looked great in the new ceramic pot and presented the feeling of a tree overhanging a cliff. Although this cultivar usually begins flowering in autumn in our cold region the best flowers can be appreciated in spring when other varieties of Dwarf and Japanese flowering quince blossom. The red cultivar is slow growing and has deep green leathery leaves.

August 1993

The fragrant small yellow fruit adds color to the design.

NO. 95 – CHOJUBAI DWARF JAPANESE FLOWERING QUINCE
Chaenomeles japonica 'Chojubai'

TOP TO BOTTOM 10 INCHES ▲ CONTAINER: AMERICAN, BRENTA SULLIVAN

MAY 2003

WILLIAM N. VALAVANIS COLLECTION
ROCHESTER, NEW YORK

no. 96 – White Chojubai Dwarf Japanese Flowering Quince

There are a few cultivars of the Chojubai dwarf Japanese flowering quince. The red cultivar is quite slow growing and has small orange red flowers and dark green foliage. The white cultivar is rare and is much more vigorous. The light green foliage is attractive but there is not much of a difference between the foliage and pale white blossoms. I have both red and white cultivars growing in my garden next to each other for study. The white cultivar seems to grow three times faster and taller than the red cultivar.

Both cultivars root easily and are winter hardy in my area.

This bonsai was started as a cutting over ten years ago and has been container grown. It formed an unusual root formation and I was not sure how to style it, so just let it grow on its own to see what would develop. In November 2011 I was leaving the Taikan ten Bonsai Exhibition in Kyoto, Japan, and spotted an unusual container under a dealer's table. It was immediately purchased and I had no idea what to plant in it or if I would ever plant in such an odd pot. I was pleasantly surprised when this White chojubai dwarf Japanese flowering quince cutting fit perfectly into the unusual container.

no. 96 – White Chojubai Dwarf Japanese Flowering Quince
Chaenomeles japonica 'Chojubai - White'

TOP TO BOTTOM 11 INCHES ▲ CONTAINER: JAPANESE TOKONAME-WARE FROM THE HOUZAN KILN

APRIL 2012

WILLIAM N. VALAVANIS COLLECTION
ROCHESTER, NEW YORK

NO. 97 – JAPANESE RED PINE

Japanese red pines are easy to grow from seed and train for bonsai. Small size bonsai can be easily created from young seedlings. It is important to begin trunk shaping early if contorted forms are desired. It is much easier to bend thin young plants, thinner than a chopstick, than older trunks the size of a cigarette.

This bonsai was started from selecting two seedlings which grew next to each other in a seed flat. They were quite close to each other so each was wired into contorted shapes and just allowed to grow. In spring the entire candle is allowed to lengthen then completely removed in early summer. The resulting new growth will have shorter needles and more branching which is best for small size bonsai.

This literati style bonsai is a bit unusual because the second smaller trunk crosses the main trunk twice. There is space between the two trunks and they are not touching. Rotating the bonsai presents different fronts, that is why I planted this bonsai in a round container.

This shohin Japanese red pine bonsai was displayed with an American suiseki in the 2008 1st U. S. National Bonsai Exhibition. There were seventy one shohin bonsai in that exhibition because of the popularity of small size trees.

NO. 97 – JAPANESE RED PINE
Pinus densiflora

HEIGHT 8 INCHES ▲ CONTAINER: JAPANESE

OCTOBER 2008

WILLIAM N. VALAVANIS COLLECTION
ROCHESTER, NEW YORK

no. 98 – Boston Ivy

This Boston ivy has foliage which is much smaller than the Boston ivy featured on page 229. The foliage is light green and delicate, not thick and heavy. Each leaf has three distinct leaflets while the other Boston ivy has a single leaf blade with three lobes.

I used the delicate characteristics of this Boston ivy to create a shohin bonsai over twenty years ago. It was started from a young seedling I found and has been completely container grown. If it were in the ground the trunk would have been huge. It is a good idea to take cuttings for future bonsai and plant them in the ground. The main display area in my bonsai garden has Boston ivy and Virginia creepers planted near the cement blocks holding up the tables. The vines grow wild covering the light grey blocks offering a bit of extra humidity during the hot summer. In autumn their foliage presents a lovely appearance. Throughout the summer we continually trim the long tendrils to keep the plants contained. At the base of each plant thick trunks are slowly developing for future bonsai.

I keep this bonsai in partial shade during the hot summer and it often produces long vines over one foot long. They are often attractive for a late summer display when placed on a tall elegant cascade table with the delicate leaves hanging down, sometimes displayed with a water pool stone.

In spring the growth of this Boston ivy is light green and compact, presenting a different feeling.

May 2009 – *The new spring growth is compact and a refreshing light green. The deeper container was used to develop a thicker trunk.*

NO. 98 – BOSTON IVY
Parthenocissus tricuspidata

TOP TO BOTTOM 6 INCHES ▲ CONTAINER: JAPANESE OLD OWARI

SEPTEMBER 2010

WILLIAM N. VALAVANIS COLLECTION
ROCHESTER, NEW YORK

NO. 99 – JAPANESE HORNBEAM

The Japanese hornbeam has large foliage, however it can be easily reduced by summer leaf cutting and by removing occasional large leaves. The foliage is pointed with pronounced veins which becomes a dependable golden color each autumn.

Although this species is grown for the interesting fruit which are produced during the summer, this small Japanese hornbeam has never flowered or fruited even though it is well over twenty years old.

This bonsai is not large, yet presents the feeling of a large deciduous tree growing in a park, which I enjoy. Each year the silhouette of the Japanese hornbeam bonsai slightly changes according to my trimming schedule.

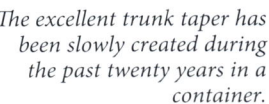

The excellent trunk taper has been slowly created during the past twenty years in a container.

NO. 99 – JAPANESE HORNBEAM
Carpinus japonica

HEIGHT 10 INCHES ▲ CONTAINER: ANTIQUE JAPANESE TOKONAME-WARE

OCTOBER 2012

WILLIAM N. VALAVANIS COLLECTION
ROCHESTER, NEW YORK

NO. 100 – WILLOW LEAF FIG

The Willow leaf fig is a popular bonsai plant cultivated in warmer areas of the world, especially in southern Florida where they can be grown outdoors all year around. In colder areas they are sturdy and can be successfully grown indoors during the winter. Heavy stems root easily and can withstand drastic pruning resulting with multiple supple new shoots. They can be grown as a small size bonsai, like this specimen, or larger size single trunk, forests and even planted on or over a rock.

This unusual shaped bonsai was found in a Florida nursery over fifteen years ago. It was pot bound and developed an odd lower trunk which interested me. It is still pot bound, yet the soil continues to drain well and the tree is well fertilized.

October 2012

The side view of the Willow leaf fig bonsai has provided the poetic name for this bonsai– "The Bashful Lady."

NO. 100 – WILLOWLEAF FIG
Ficus salicaria

HEIGHT 14 INCHES ▲ CONTAINER: CHINESE XIXING-WARE

OCTOBER 2012

WILLIAM N. VALAVANIS COLLECTION
ROCHESTER, NEW YORK

Bonsai Displays & Garden

Alcove Bonsai Displays

Spring Alcove Display – *Golden full moon maple with Dwarf iris.*

Summer Alcove Display – *Kashima Japanese maple displayed with suiseki in a water basin for the hot summer season.*

Autumn Alcove Display – *Rough bark Japanese maple displayed with Japanese forest grass and Princess persimmon.*

Winter Alcove Display – *Kashima Japanese maple displayed with suiseki in a daiza for the winter season with Sargent juniper.*

Bonsai Garden Views

Spring Bonsai Table – *Colorful maple bonsai leafing out contrast with the dark green pine bonsai.*

Autumn Bonsai Table – *The colorful Dancing peacock full moon maple garden tree frames the bonsai changing color.*

Summer View – *The different shades of green are refreshing during the summer and are waiting for their autumn coloring.*

Spring View – *Rough bark Japanese maple leafing out with fresh leaves.*

Summer View – *Rough bark Japanese maple with bright green leaves.*

Autumn View – *Rough bark Japanese maple in orange autumn glory.*

Winter View – *Rough bark Japanese maple covered with fresh snow.*

Profile

The eldest of three sons, William N. Valavanis was born on September 3, 1951 in Waukegan, Illinois, to Nicholas and Irene Valavanis, first generation Greek-Americans.

Bill displayed an early interest in nature that was stimulated by his mother's love and skill in gardening. In the early 1960s, his mother and her gardening buddy went to a bonsai demonstration where they each received a free Japanese yew to "try for bonsai." Bill was "dragged along" for the trip, and this began his lifelong passion for bonsai.

He eagerly sought information and tried to shape plants into primitive bonsai. During an exploratory nature hike along the shore of Lake Michigan, he once collected hundreds of small "pine seedlings" and individually planted them. Later he learned that his pine seedlings were actually pieces of club moss. In 1966 the Valavanis family moved to Charleston, West Virginia where Bill explored the beautiful hillsides and came home with plants for bonsai and numerous cases of poison ivy.

In 1967, at the age of sixteen, he began lecturing to garden clubs in the Charleston area. Encouraged to sell and teach bonsai, his business "The House Of Bonsai" was established. The Valavanis family moved to Rochester, New York, in 1968, along with many bonsai and pets. Bill still showed the unusual "single interest in bonsai," despite the advice of others to take a "broader view of life" and seek other interests. His parents, however, continued to stimulate and encourage him to pursue his interest in bonsai.

Bill graduated from the State University Of New York at Farmingdale, Long Island, in 1971, majoring in Ornamental Horticulture. He became an active member and Director of the Bonsai Society Of Greater New York and attended classes with Yuji Yoshimura in Tarrytown, New York on weekends. While still at college his first mail order catalog was published in 1970 listing numerous bonsai starter stock and chrysanthemums for bonsai.

During the summer of 1970, encouraged by Lynn Perry, who helped make arrangements, Bill went to Japan to study bonsai with Kyuzo Murata at Kyuka-en Bonsai Garden in Omiya, Japan. He also began studying saikei with Toshio Kawamoto at the Nippon Bonsai-Saikei Institute in Tokyo.

After returning home he sold most of his bonsai collection to finance a longer apprenticeship in Japan. From 1971 to 1972 Bill studied with Kakutaro Komuro at Shoto-en Bonsai Garden in Omiya, Japan. He continued his studies with Toshio Kawamoto and took classes on bonsai chrysanthemums with Tameji Nakajima. To learn more about Japanese design and line, he studied the "Shofu School" of Ikebana receiving a master's teaching certificate.

Returning home from Japan he began teaching regular bonsai classes in Rochester and traveling throughout the United States and Canada teaching classical bonsai art. In 1974, he enrolled at Cornell University majoring in Floriculture and Ornamental Horticulture, and still continued his business and teaching activities in Rochester.

After graduation in 1976 he lived, studied and taught bonsai courses with Yuji Yoshimura at the Yoshimura School Of Bonsai in Briarcliff Manor, New York. A thirty year study and relationship with Mr. Yoshimura has provided him with the background, knowledge and enthusiasm to promote classical bonsai art.

In 1978, he was Editor for one year of *The Bonsai Bulletin,* published by The Bonsai Society Of Greater New York, as well as a Director of the organization.

In 1978, he changed the name of his business from The House Of Bonsai to The International Bonsai Arboretum, to reflect his new goals and ambitions. His life was now dedicated to the promotion of the international artistic and horticultural expression of classical bonsai art through propagation and education throughout the world. Bill has introduced, propagated and popularized many plants including yatsubusa, dwarf and unusual cultivars of pine, maple, elm, quince and porcelain berry.

In order to reach the greatest number of English speaking bonsai fanciers, he began publishing *International BONSAI* in 1979, now reaching over fifty countries. This magazine was the first and only professional bonsai magazine published in the United States. He sponsored over thirty symposia in Rochester were sponsored which attracted people from around the world because of the educational programs, instructors and organization.

He has authored many articles which have been printed in English, Japanese and European publications in addition to *The Encyclopedia Of Classical Bonsai Art, Volumes I & II,* which are now out of print. He has made TV appearances in North America, Japan, Korea, Italy and Australia.

In 1987 Bill married Diane McAleer from Montreal, Canada, and they have two sons, Nicholas and Christopher. Together they moved The International Bonsai Arboretum to a larger location in the Rochester area where they continue to offer a full curriculum of classical bonsai art classes.

Yuji Yoshimura teaching William N. Valavanis in 1969.

William N. Valavanis with his bonsai collection in 1966.

Bill has made well over fifty trips to Japan to study and lead bonsai tours. His teaching travels have covered England, South America, China, Indonesia, Japan, Taiwan, Belgium, Italy, Australia as well as North America.

In April 2006 the Chinese government invited him, a Greek American to travel to China to teach Japanese bonsai art, which the Chinese invented. In 2007 he presented a two day demonstration at the Ginkgo Award Exhibition in Belgium and was also a demonstrator at the 2012 Noelanders Cup Exhibition.

He assisted in establishing The Bonsai Society Of Upstate New York in the Rochester area which still remains one of the most active and distinguished organizations on the east coast. Ten years ago the organization celebrated their thirty anniversary and presented Bill with a "Lifetime Achievement Award" for his forty years of dedication and accomplishments to the art of bonsai.

In 2003 the officers and directors of the American Bonsai Society also presented him with the Distinguished Lifetime Achievement Award in recognition and gratitude for outstanding contributions as scholar, author, publisher, creative artist, teacher, symposium organizer, tour guide and international ambassador of good will, and for many years of service dedication and friendship to the American Bonsai Society.

His bonsai masterpieces are often featured in English and foreign bonsai books and periodicals, often on covers. He continues to share his knowledge with non-profit organizations and is a Director of the National Bonsai Foundation. In the Rochester area Bill is on the steering committee of GardenScape and produces award winning bonsai garden displays each spring for their garden show.

Suiseki, bonsai reference books and lapel pins are also passions of Bill and he has contributed to their understanding and promotion around the world. His bonsai reference library is extensive with many old Japanese books and magazines, including Yuji Yoshimura's personal collection.

In 2008 he organized the historic 1ST U. S. National Bonsai Exhibition which was successful and drew visitors from around the world. The 2ND and 3RD U.S. National Bonsai exhibition were held in 2010 and 2012. The 4TH U. S. National Bonsai Exhibition will be held on September 13-14, 2014.

He freely shares his fifty years of dedicated bonsai passion, study, experiences and discoveries with students and serious bonsai fanciers through *International BONSAI* and his educational bonsai programs. Bill continues to strive for excellence through his dedication to promoting classical bonsai on an international scale.

William N. Valavanis with his bonsai collection in 1993.

William N. Valavanis with his bonsai collection in 2003.

Mr. and Mrs. Kyuzo Murata, left, with daughter-in-law Rumiko, appreciating photos of bonsai by William N. Valavanis in June 1985. The summer of 1970 was spent studying with Kyuzo Murata at Kyuka-en Bonsai Garden in Omiya Bonsai Village, Japan.

William N. Valavanis teaching advanced bonsai pine pruning techniques to long time students, left to right, Harvey Carapella, Paul Eschmann, Roy Wixson and Rick Marriott in 2011. Small study groups are an excellent way to teach bonsai.

Teaching & Sharing Bonsai Information & Techniques

October 2009 – *10TH Asia-Pacific Bonsai & Suiseki Convention & Exhibition demonstration on Japanese five-needle pine bonsai in Taichung, Taiwan.*

June 2012 – *Opening Ceremony at the 2012 3rd U. S. National Bonsai Exhibition held in Rochester, New York.*

September 2011 – *The Bonsai Society Of Western Australia Classical Bonsai Art Seminar in Perth, Australia, consisted of several demonstrations critique and workshops.*

September 2011 – *The 3rd African Bonsai Convention featured several demonstrations and workshops in Durban, South Africa. A large near-view forest of Trident maples was created.*

1972 - Present – *Educational bonsai courses, seminars, workshops, tours and demonstrations are conducted each spring, summer and autumn at the International Bonsai Arboretum in Rochester, New York using the extensive bonsai collection and display accessories.*

August 2007 – *A bonsai demonstration was presented at the 9ᵀᴴ Asia Pacific Bonsai & Suiseki Convention in Bali, Indonesia.*

November 2008 – *During a tour to Japan a special Display Seminar was organized and conducted by Kunio Kobayashi and Peter Warren at the Shunka-en Bonsai Museum in Tokyo, Japan.*

Publications

The Encyclopedia Of Bonsai Art: Volume 1
Bonsai Creation And Design Using Propagation Techniques
Symmes Systems, 1975.

The Encyclopedia Of Bonsai Art: Volume 2
Japanese Five-needle Pine: Nature Gardens, Bonsai, Taxonomy
Symmes Systems, 1976.

International BONSAI Magazine
First and only professional bonsai magazine published in the United States
Premier issue Spring 1979 – 2013/2, 138 issues.

Bonsai: Past – Present – Future
Commemorating 30 Years Of Bonsai By William N. Valavanis
1993.

Forest, Rock Plantings & Ezo Spruce Bonsai **By Saburo Kato**
Edited & Compiled
National Bonsai Foundation, Inc. 2001.

Bonsai: Past – Present – Future
Commemorating 40 Years Of Bonsai By William N. Valavanis
2003.

1ˢᵀ U. S. National Bonsai Exhibition Commemorative Album
2008.

2ᴺᴰ U. S. National Bonsai Exhibition Commemorative Album
2010.

3ᴿᴰ U. S. National Bonsai Exhibition Commemorative Album
2012.

Fine Bonsai: Art & Nature
Co-authored with Jonathan Singer
Abbeville Press, 2012.

May 2009 – *Several demonstrations and critiques were presented at the Australian National Bonsai Convention in Brisbane, Australia.*

April 2006 – *A Powerpoint presentation began a demonstration on classical bonsai at the 2006 International Penjing & Shangshi Expo held in Chencun, China.*

November 2012 – *Several bonsai demonstrations and critiques were presented at the Northern Brazil Bonsai Conference in Fortaleza, Brazil.*

January 2012 – *Two demonstrations were presented at the 13ᵀᴴ Noelanders Award Exhibition held in Heusden-Zolder, Belgium. Corin Tomlinson from England a graduate apprentice came to assist.*

Colophon

Camera:
Hasselbald 500c
Carl Zeiss 50mm Distagon lens
Carl Zeiss 80mm Planar Lens
Phase One p25 Digital Back
Canon EOS 7D
Canon EFS 15-85mm Lens

Lighting:
Calumet Genenis 200 & 750 electronic Strobe
LiteLink Radio Trigger System

Color Management:
X-Rite i1 Extreem Spectrophotometer
X-Rite i1 Profiler software
X-Rite i1 Publish software

Computers:
Apple Mac Pro Duo Quad 8 Core
Apple Mac Pro Quad Core
Apple Macbook Pro

Software:
Adobe Photoshop CS5 version 12.0.4
Adobe Camera Raw 7.3
Capture One Pro 7.1 Software
Imagenomic NoiseWare 5
Nik Software Viveza 2.0.09
Adobe InDesign CS4
Micrsoft Word 2008 Mac
Adobe Acrobat Professional
OnOne Perfect Resize 7.0 Professional Edition
SilverFast 8 Scanning Software
Topaz In Focus

Typeface Body type:
Minion Pro-Regular, Bold, Italic

Typeface Headings:
Minion Pro- Semibold Italic

Proofing:
Hewlett Packer LaserJet p2055dn
Lanier Color Multifunction ld520c
Epson Stylus Photo R2880
Epson Ultra Chrome K3 Ink
Kirkland Professioinal Glossy Inkjet Photo

Paper:
128 gsm Glossy Artpaper

Printing Press:
Heidleberg Speedmaster

Printer:
WKT Co. Ltd./Zebra IP

Binding:
Sewn, Endpapered, Square case, Jacketed